Ella Rodman Church

Money-making for ladies

Ella Rodman Church
Money-making for ladies
ISBN/EAN: 9783744737326
Printed in Europe, USA, Canada, Australia, Japan
Cover: Foto ©Lupo / pixelio.de

More available books at **www.hansebooks.com**

MONEY-MAKING

FOR

LADIES

BY
ELLA RODMAN CHURCH

NEW YORK
HARPER & BROTHERS, FRANKLIN SQUARE
1882

Entered according to Act of Congress, in the year 1882, by

HARPER & BROTHERS,

In the Office of the Librarian of Congress, at Washington.

All rights reserved.

INTRODUCTION.

"I wish I knew how to make some money!" says Ysolte of the white hands, and she sighs with a feeling of utter incapacity as she says it.

She has possibly painted some marine views on large, white clam-shells, and offered them to a shopkeeper to be disposed of on commission, under cover of a thick veil, and with a guilty manner that half roused the man's suspicions as to whether, like the wares of the brushmaker who undersold his neighbor, they had not been stolen ready-made.

Ysolte sympathizes with the crumpet-woman who, when crying her wares, hoped to goodness no one heard her; but the public generally do not seem to appreciate works of art on clam-shell backgrounds—at least, that portion of the public who frequent Mr. Jones's stationery shop; and the Decorative Art Society is equally unenlightened, having declined them with a kind note advising the artist to study Art!

What, then, shall Ysolte do? Her case is undoubtedly hard—she is totally destitute of a new silk dress, the means to purchase Christmas presents, and various other comforts and belongings of civilized life; but hope may, perhaps, be found for her, and for others of that numerous class who, while not obliged to enter the ranks of recognized working-women, strongly feel the need of increasing a limited income.

"People want things to do," said some one lately, "and yet there are a hundred practicable things undone to-day, for want of some one to do them."

It seems only necessary to bring the two together; and some of the suggestions offered in this little volume may be found useful by those who are not satisfied with being poor and not fitted for hard work.

CONTENTS.

Chapter I.

THE BOARDING-HOUSE QUESTION.

Competition. — Improved Methods. — A Lady's Resource. — Requisites for Success. — Short-sightedness of Landladies. — An Inviting Table. — A Refined Home. — Boarding-houses for Workingmen..Page 13

Chapter II.

THE HOUSE-KEEPER'S OPPORTUNITIES.

Putting up Preserves for Sale.—Sources for Disposing of them.—Quality and Economy.—Popular Kinds. —Care in Small Things. — Best Methods of Preserving.—Low-priced Goods.—Room Higher Up.— Showy and Economical Jars. — Brandied. Fruit.— Jellies.—Marmalades.—A Lady's Success.......... 28

Chapter III.

THE HOUSE-KEEPER'S OPPORTUNITIES (Continued).

Demand and Supply.—"With *brains*, sir!"—The Pies of Boyhood.—"Money in it."—Advantages of Home-

made Pies.—A Waiting Market.—"Apple Pye."
—Good Bread.—The Country Baker.—A New Departure.—Modest Beginnings.—Cheap Restaurants.
—An Unsupplied Want.—A Bright Idea.—The Ladies' Lunch-room.—Division of Labor.—Coffee at
the Sea-shore.—A Money-making Scheme.—Confectionery for Watering-places....................Page 44

Chapter IV.

WHAT MAY BE DONE WITH THE NEEDLE.

Use and Abuse of the Needle.—Ladies' Depositories.
—A Museum of Fancy-work.—Judgment and Invention.—Society of Decorative Art.—Quaint Productions.—Profitable but Unattractive Work.—Indian Bead-work.—An Old Woman's Emery-bags.—
A Monopoly Desirable.—Small Inventions.—Knitting and Crocheting.—Dress-making and Millinery.
—Convenience and Economy.—Travelling Advantages.—Pins vs. Needles.—Home Dress-making.—
An Easy Way of Learning.—Private Remunerative
Work.—A Lady's Experiment.—Observation and
Ingenuity.—A Neglected Art.—An Establishment
for Repairs... 60

Chapter V.

TEACHING IN ITS VARIOUS BRANCHES.

The Profession of Teaching.—"Classes and Lessons."
—Ordinary Remuneration.—A Class in Literature.
—A Few Suggestions.—The Study of Botany.—
Reading Aloud.—Ordinary Failings.—Reading to

an Invalid.—Music Lessons.—A Modern Cecilia.—Appreciation.—Instruction in Fancy-work.—A Sewing-school.—A Class in Mending.—An Object to Work for.—Cooking-schools.—Teaching as an Exchange ....Page 77

CHAPTER VI.

LITERATURE AND WRITING.

"Prose and Worse."—Undeveloped Talent.—Mistaken Ideas.—Some Open Doors.—A Mercenary View of the Subject.—What to Write About.—Rates of Remuneration.—Literary Giants.—Century Plants.—What an Author Needs.—Novel Writing a Trade.—Works of Fiction.—Profits of Periodical Literature.—Elements of Success.—Value of Advertising.—Sensational Writers.—A Lady's Attempt with a Dime Novel.—Sunday-school Books.—A List of Periodicals.—Writing by Proxy.—Advertisements.—Letter-writing.—Legal Copying.—Book-keeping.. 90

CHAPTER VII.

ART INDUSTRIES.

Schools of Design.—Fundamental Instruction.—Impossible Achievements.—Practical Skill in Designing.—Mechanical Drawing.—Women as Architects.—Engraving on Gold and Silver.—The New York Society of Decorative Art.—Objects of the Society.—A Depot for First-class Work.—Conditions for Exhibitors.—China Painting.—The Decoration of

Fans.—Hand-screens, Plaques, etc.—Door-panels.—Illustrations for Books.—A Superfluity of Genius..Page 110

Chapter VIII.

HOUSE-DECORATION.

Two English Ladies.—The Decorator of the Past.—A New Field for Women of Taste and Judgment.—The Woman's Province.—How to Begin.—Conscientious Work.—A "House Beautiful."—Farther Suggestions.—A Pair of Vases........................ 128

Chapter IX.

SHOPPING ON COMMISSION.—AGENCIES.

Attractions of Shopping on Commission.—Profits Received.—Reasons for Decline.—Comparative Advantages of New York and other Places.—Necessary Qualifications.—Suggestions for a Circular.—Advertisements.—Shopping for Friends.—Book Agents.—A City Lady's Enterprise.—Characteristics of Agents.—Encouragement for Ladies.—Miss G——'s Experience.—The Catastrophe.—A Decided Contrast.—Munificent Emoluments.—Other Subscription-works.—An Agent by Proxy.—Small Wares.—Advantages of Knowing how to Work. 137

Chapter X.

GARDENING FOR PROFIT.

Advantages of a Country Residence.—Value of a Garden-patch.—What Has Been Done.—Want of Enterprise.—A Small Garden Well Managed.—What a Woman Might Do.—Opportunities in Fruit-raising.—The Capabilities of Currants.—A Condensed Strawberry Farm.—How to Start and Manage it.—Quinces to the Front.—Advantages and Drawbacks.—Fruit-growing Generally .... Page 159

Chapter XI.

AMONG THE FLOWERS.

Scarcity of Women Florists.—First Steps.—Building a Greenhouse.—Economical Plans.—Variety not Desirable.—A Rose Garden under Glass.—Exterminating Insects.—Heliotrope.—A Market for Cut Flowers.—Ferns, Autumn Leaves, Grasses, etc.—A Corner Ornament.. 178

Chapter XII.

BEES AND POULTRY.

Recommendations of Bee-culture.—Profit in Keeping Bees.—A Lady's Testimony.—Two Western Girls.—How to Prevent Stinging.—"How am I to Begin?"—Swarming Prevented.—Wintering Bees.—Making Honey from Sugar.—Pink Honey.—Profits from Hens.—Accommodation for Poultry.—General Care.—A Frenchwoman's Experience.—Roses and Honeysuckles.—French Soil.—Horse-flesh as Food.—Artificial Hatching.—The Barn-yard Fowl.—A Paying Business.—Rules for Successful Poultry-raising.—Spring Chickens.—Pigeons.—Proper Shelter.—Dutchies, or Common Runts, most Profitable.

—A Flock of Turkeys.—Causes of Failure.—Delicacy of Young Turkeys.—Carefulness in Feeding.—Ducks and Geese............................Page 188

Chapter XIII.

A FEW LAST WORDS.

The Value of Small Things.—Suggestions in Newspaper Paragraphs.—A Novel Pattern for an Auger.—Oyster and Snail Shells.—Improved Milk and Butter.—Profit in Tea-packing.—A Little Tea Store.—Cultivation of Mushrooms.—A Lady's Invention.—A Need to be Supplied.—Knowing What to Do.—Wasted Energy................................... 216

MONEY-MAKING FOR LADIES.

Chapter I.

THE BOARDING-HOUSE QUESTION.

Competition.—Improved Methods.—A Lady's Resource.—Requisites for Success.—Short-sightedness of Landladies.—An Inviting Table.—A Refined Home.—Boarding-houses for Working-men.

Most of the popular roads to money-making are crowded with competitors; and those who would find what they want are obliged to turn into by-paths and make their own roads as they go. Sometimes the desired end is accomplished by doing a thing that has long been badly done in a more satisfactory way; and the occupation of taking boarders will serve to illustrate this theory.

The average lady thrown upon her own resources, especially if she have what is known in such cases as "a roof over her head," is almost sure to take boarders; and, with the "roof" secured, she may, if fortunate in her inmates, feel tolerably sure of a comfortable living. But to take boarders as a sole dependence for obtaining the necessaries of life is as precarious and harassing an occupation as can possibly be found; especially with the risk of hiring a large house and furnishing it for the purpose. The case is not so difficult with the occupant of her own house, who, having a room or rooms that can very well be spared, chooses to diminish her household expenses by adding to the number of her family. It increases her cares also, but money cannot be made in *any* way without effort of some kind; and this is one that seems preferable to many others.

To succeed, however, in keeping boarders, either on a large or a small scale, requires good house-keeping and a certain talent for economy — which does not mean providing poor things, but getting the most for one's money. An economical house-keeper, who understands her business, will furnish a good table for a sum which, in the hands of one who thinks only of saving money, will produce the most unsatisfactory results. The manner of cooking and serving food has quite as much to do with its attractiveness as the quality of the purchases; and badly-cooked meats and vegetables can never be made inviting, whatever their original cost may have been.

There is frequently a kind of airy unconcern about those who take boarders, in regard to all matters not absolutely down in the bond, which is highly exasperating; and, considering all things, the wonder is not that so many fail in this calling, but that any succeed. Were it not that there is always an abundant supply of homeless people in the world—people who are homeless from necessity, and people who are homeless from choice — landladies who trouble themselves only about bare necessities would oftener find that "it did not pay to take boarders."

Where, for instance, does one engaged in looking for board chance to light upon a room that has anything of a *home look* about it? Do not the apartments shown rather convey the idea that some one has just died there, and everything been dismantled in consequence? Not a bit of drapery to bed or windows—not a bracket or a table-cover—not a cushion or footstool. The four walls are there—generally with an ugly paper on them; the regulation bedstead, bureau, and chairs;

possibly a hard lounge, but probably none at all. What possibilities of cheerfulness are there in such a room, provided the unfortunate occupants have no embellishments of their own with which to enliven it?

"But we cannot afford to ornament rooms," say the struggling landladies; "it wouldn't pay; we can hardly make both ends meet as it is."

This is just where they make a mistake; because it *would* pay. It would pay to drape the windows with cheap but tasteful curtains of white muslin or cretonne, Canton-flannel, or low-priced worsted stuff—to drape the mantel with the same, and to have a table-cover to match or harmonize. A lounge could be improvised from a packing-box, furnished with springs and a small hair-mattress, and covered to match the draperies. A few touches of this kind would completely transform an ugly room into a noticeably pretty one; and the small outlay required would prove an excellent investment.

The proprietor of a small boarding-house was lately advised by a friend, temporarily occupying a large room which the landlady was vainly trying to dispose of permanently, to make a few such improvements before applicants came to inspect it, window-curtains of some kind being particularly recommended.

"Oh, I *mean* to get them, if any one takes the room," was the reply; "but as long as there is no money coming in, I can't afford to spend anything on an uncertainty."

Her friend endeavored to convince her that an outlay of ten dollars on the spacious, bare-looking room would be returned tenfold, but all to no purpose. The bedstead and bureau were of walnut, while the chairs and small side-table were maple; but "when the room was taken," the landlady said, the furniture would be properly matched, the other walnut articles being then in some other part of the house.

The room was not taken; and, in all probability, the head of that house will never succeed in keeping boarders or in any other occupation.

A lady who desires to increase her income by receiving, perhaps, one inmate into her family will find no difficulty, if she resides in a city, in obtaining an unexceptionable lady or gentleman boarder, who is willing to pay liberally for the comforts of a refined home. There are many such persons who detest boarding-houses, and would gladly dispense with a great variety of viands, for the sake of having what *is* put on the table made inviting. Even so simple a dish as the popular ante-breakfast course of oatmeal is seldom cooked so as to be fit to eat. Often brought to the table half raw, because so few cooks seem to understand the immense amount of moderate boiling, or simmering, that it requires, it quite deserves the name of "chicken-feed," by which it is facetiously designated. It *can* be made, however, a very delicate and nourishing dish, if served with cream or good rich milk.

It is not necessary in this connection to go into the details of breakfast, dinner, and tea—a passing allusion to the characteristics of a successful boarding-house being all that is required. The assertion can be easily proved from facts that the people who are fruitlessly seeking for home-like quarters are far more numerous than those who have such quarters to offer. It follows, therefore, that any lady who will furnish something more attractive than usual will have no cause to complain of want of success.

The only kind of boarding-house which a *lady* can conduct comfortably in person is one that provides a refined home for those who are willing to pay for its privileges, and who prefer it to the care of a home of their own. Half a dozen rooms with inmates of this class —two or three, perhaps, being rented *en suite*—would bring a much handsomer profit, with far less care, than if the number were doubled and filled with impecunious clerks and struggling young married couples.

There should be no threadbare carpets, nor shabby nor sham articles of any kind, in this model boarding-house of ours; an air of quiet elegance and general well-to-do-ativeness should pervade the establishment throughout;

there should be an immaculate front entrance, a stand of trailing and growing plants in the vestibule, a handsome umbrella and hat stand, *portières*, if you please, to the parlor door-ways, and an inhabited look to the parlors themselves; for there would be no caravan of Goths and Vandals, in the shape of third and fourth rate boarders, to pour through the house and destroy things, but wellbred inmates, who would appreciate their advantages too highly to injure them.

It seems strange to the careful observer that so little provision, except in the way of exorbitant charges, has been made for this class; and tastefully-furnished rooms and a well-appointed table are too seldom offered to justify the hasty conclusion that they do not pay. We feel sure that they *would* pay—for such rooms and such a table would command almost any price within the bounds of reason; and the six or eight people grouped around the board, arranged as if for a small dinner-party, with nothing visible but the central stand of flowers and the ornamental dessert—while the well-trained waiter quietly carves the meats at a side-table, and presents the dishes to the guests—the lady of the house sitting at the head of her table, handsomely dressed, and free from all anxiety, would feel that a full equivalent was rendered them for a very handsome outlay.

Humbler boarding-houses well-conducted, and especially in manufacturing places, would not fail to be appreciated; and clean, comfortable rooms, tastefully arranged (for the cheapest things may be tasteful), with plain, wholesome food, nicely cooked, and varied as much as possible, could be made to pay handsomely. The boarders should not be able to say, "Wednesday is always corned-beef-and-cabbage day;" or, "Friday, we are sure to have fish—only this, and nothing more;" a regular routine of viands is inexpressibly wearisome, and may easily be avoided by a little good management.

A lady, some years ago, found herself reduced, by the death of her husband, from affluence to poverty, and left with several small children to be supported by the work of her own unaided head and hands. She would consider no proposals from friends that she should open a fashionable boarding-house; but, selecting a plain good-sized dwelling in the right neighborhood, she managed to secure it, probably on the strength of her own well-known character, and fitted it up with a view to the especial class of people whom she expected to receive as boarders.

This was the class of mechanics, and single men were not only "preferred," but insisted on; and as soon as one of the inmates married, his place in the establishment was forfeited. A dozen others were always ready to step into it; for Mrs. D——'s boarding-house was so admirably conducted, that waiting hosts of outside working-men turned longing eyes toward it. The adjoining house was speedily added to the first one, and as speedily filled; and, in the course of a few years, the enterprising landlady owned them both, and was enabled to educate her children thoroughly, and even to lay up money for their future needs.

The question naturally arises, how did this one woman manage to succeed in an enterprise that would seem so little suited to a lady, and the details of which she could scarcely be expected to grasp understandingly? Practical good-sense and quick powers of observation supplied in Mrs. D——'s case the lack of experience; and she furnished at reasonable prices an abundance of plain, excellent fare, with rooms that could be comfortably lived in, instead of being used only as sleeping-bunks—for even busy working-men can appreciate neatness and harmonious coloring.

This lady chose to preside in her own dining-room, and even attended to the carving, with the aid of an assistant; and the respectful greeting of each man, as he entered and took his seat, was an instinctive recognition of the claims of his landlady on his deference and consideration.

An establishment of this kind might be conducted, through a trustworthy deputy, without the appearance of the real head of the house; but Mrs. D——

was none the less a lady because she preferred managing her business in person, while her expenses were less, and her plans more thoroughly carried out, than if she had hired a substitute.

Chapter II.

THE HOUSE-KEEPER'S OPPORTUNITIES.

Putting up Preserves for Sale.—Sources for Disposing of them.—Quality and Economy.—Popular Kinds. —Care in Small Things.—Best Methods of Preserving.—Low-priced Goods.—Room Higher Up.— Showy and Economical Jars.—Brandied Fruit.— Jellies.—Marmalades.—A Lady's Success.

MANY branches of industry that can be pursued in a quiet way suggest themselves in connection with house-keeping; and the would-be money-maker who has a house of her own will find it a comparatively easy matter to carry out her object. Why should not the carefully-prepared delicacies so lavishly displayed on the table of the ambitious house-keeper for the admiration of her friends also be converted into a source of revenue?

Preserved and canned fruits are especially available; "store preserves" are generally insipid, and canned peaches from the same source are sure to require more sugar, as well as more cooking, before they are fit for the table. As sugar is a formidable item of expense in putting up fruit, it is natural for those who are trying to keep what they have and get all they can, to scant it; while the less cooking the fruit gets, the larger and firmer it appears. Preserves that are free from these defects, and yet manufactured at nearly the same cost, can scarcely fail to find a ready market as soon as their merits are known; and a lady without much ready money to risk could easily try half a dozen jars, which she could use for home consumption, in the event of their not being disposed of.

A wise preliminary step would be to consult some dealer in such articles as to the demand for preserves, the most popular kinds, and the profit to be expected. City confectioners and dealers in foreign fruits, etc., have opportunities for disposing of such delicacies, and will, in most cases, be quite willing to undertake it on a reasonable commission. A country store might possibly do even better, as there would be little danger of competition; and in some neighborhoods, where the residents are able to indulge in luxuries, the novelty would be so great, as well as the relief to house-keepers, that such an occupation, if conducted with skill and care, could soon be made very remunerative.

In every case, however, where it is possible, the business should be transacted between the producer and the consumer, to avoid the payment of a commission to any third party, which makes quite a serious difference in the profits. Friends are sometimes sufficiently numerous and liberal to prevent the need of seeking customers among outside parties; and in this way, without any publicity, a lady will receive as many orders for preserves as she can conveniently attend to.

The question has been asked, while this book was in progress, "Cannot good preserves be bought cheaper than they can be made?" And various instances were cited, and one well-known firm in particular mentioned, of marvellously low prices and unexceptionable preserves. It is not to be supposed that ladies are advised in these pages to enter into competition with the large canning and preserving establishments that do their work by machinery, and fill every market with it at very moderate prices, but merely to produce superior home-made articles for a home market.

There are customers to be found who

willingly pay a higher price for apparently the same article that is offered elsewhere at a considerable discount; but, when bought even at the best of the large establishments, they cannot feel as sure of pure materials and proper modes of cooking as when taken from a private manufacturer, whose success depends upon these very points. Most of the preserves, too, that are publicly offered for sale have a fine outward appearance, but a most insipid taste; while the purchaser of cheap *brandied* fruits runs a fearful risk of disease, and even death, from the injurious effects of the cheap spirits employed in their manufacture. *Good* brandied fruits cannot be made cheaply, for the reason that good fruits and good brandy are not to be had for next to nothing; and those who have the sense to know this prefer buying such wares at higher rates of a person who will make them conscientiously.

But they can be made understandingly as well; and the lady who is engaged in preserving may have some friend whose business relations will enable him to procure her materials at wholesale rates. This lightens the expense in some degree, though not so much, with *good* articles, as may generally be supposed; and the poet's well-known line,

"Earth gets its price for what earth gives us,"

is quite applicable here.

The judicious use of *ammonia* has been recommended as a perfectly legitimate way of reducing the expense of sugar in preserving, as this ingredient is quite harmless, and does not affect the appearance of the fruit, when properly used. In the course of boiling, a small quantity should be stirred in and the effect carefully noted. The alkali of the ammonia combines with the acid of the fruit, producing a neutral reaction which permits the sugar to have its full effect. If too much ammonia finds its way in, the addition of a little vinegar will remedy the excess.

With regard to fruit, happy is she who can say, even if it *is* a travesty,

"I know a bank where the wild *raspberry* grows;"

for the preserving capabilities of this insignificant-looking fruit are infinite, and it has the advantage over the cultivated berry of belonging to any one who will take the trouble of gathering it. Raspberry jam affords an inexhaustible store for puddings, tarts, jelly-cake, ices, etc., and one can scarcely make too much of it. Raspberry jelly and raspberry sirup are also popular; and the rich, beautiful color of all these compounds is as pleasing to the eye as the taste is to the palate.

Blackberries, too, are valuable in their way, though somewhat unpleasantly seedy, and are quite popular in the shape of jam and jelly and sirup. Strawberry preserves are always welcome; peaches are taken for granted; the dark-blue plums are a delightful combination of tart and sweet. But the latter are seldom offered for sale in the shape of preserves; and with the fullest of purses one cannot easily buy quince marmalade. Guava marmalade, which has to be brought from the tropics, is comparatively common; but certain home preserves are still waiting for some enterprising woman to put their separate materials together, and create a demand by furnishing a supply.

To manufacture an article a little differently, or to put it up in a peculiarly attractive form, is almost sure to prove a successful enterprise; and, especially in the matter of preserving, superior workmanship and original devices will always bring in satisfactory returns.

"The French," says a recent writer on the subject, "make the clearest, best preserves, because they spare no pains. They first prepare their sirup or clarified sugar; then, after neatly and carefully paring or dressing their fruit, cook a few pieces at a time, or only as many as they can oversee, carefully lifting each piece out of the sirup the moment it is done. To make clear, good preserves requires, first, no economy of trouble; second, that the fruit be perfectly fresh— *alive* from the tree or bush, or, as a friend says, 'tasting of the sun.'"

Some persons talk of "having good-luck with preserves;" but the good-luck will almost invariably be found to result from care and experience. A little originality, too, goes a great way; but experiments out of the beaten track should be made with great caution. A little may be gleaned here and there from books, as well as from practical house-keepers; and, after carefully laying the foundations, the business might be commenced on a small scale.

It must be remembered, however, that it is one in which there is great competition—the market being fairly flooded with low-priced goods that are not *cheap* because of so inferior a quality; and that only by providing something better than usual, at fairly reasonable rates, can any one now entering the field hope to make the occupation of preserving at all profitable. For those who will do this kind of work there is much encouragement; and a quotation from a volume for business men is quite in place here:

"A wide range of opportunity for fortune is open to men of enterprise, even in the beaten tracks of commerce, by an improvement in the quality of common and ordinary articles of export, and in the modes of shipping them. By a little persevering examination you will readily discover articles which, by extra care in sending out only the best qualities, and put up in such a manner that they will retain their quality when they arrive, will be certain to bring back satisfactory returns."

"There is always room higher up," even in the preserving business; and the Exchange for Woman's Work, in New York, which disposes of the best class of such goods on commission, says in its report that the market only waits to be supplied—whatever is *really good* is sold, and there is a clamorous call for more.

In putting up preserves the clearest and whitest jars should be selected, as the fruit is then displayed to the best advantage; and, although tin cans have the advantage of keeping their contents so perfectly air-tight that fermentation is impossible, they are very inferior in appearance to the glass bottles, and not satisfactory to the purchaser, who is thus prevented from seeing the goods without opening them. The ordinary glass canning jars, sold as quarts and pints, consume an inordinate amount of fruit, if put in at all closely; and the best and most ornamental receptacles are the French bottles—also called quarts, but not requiring so much to fill them—which can probably be obtained from the large wholesale dealers in such wares.

One dollar and fifty cents per quart jar is the current price for superior brandied fruit, while ordinary preserves sell somewhat lower; but when any kind of fruit is scarce and dear, the price of that particular kind of preserve must advance in proportion.

Jellies of almost every kind are salable, and for *currant* jelly especially there is a constant demand, as it is indispensable with game and venison. Nothing, perhaps, affords a better illustration than currant jelly of the advantages to be derived from doing a thing in the best possible manner, and then putting it up in an attractive shape. Red and white currants mixed make the prettiest color; and in some cases it would pay to make the white and red separately, and let it harden in alternate layers in the receptacles. This makes it very ornamental for the table, and such moulds would probably be in demand for dinner-parties.

Clearness and color are, of course, essentials in jelly-making, and to secure the desired results every detail must be carefully attended to. These begin with the picking of the fruit; and it is advised to "gather the fruit early, as soon as fully ripe, since the pulp softens and the juice is less rich if allowed to remain long after ripening. In our climate, the first week in July is usually considered the time to make currant jelly. Never gather currants or other soft or small seed fruit immediately after rain, for preserving purposes, as they are greatly impoverished by the moisture absorbed."

Marmalades, and especially those made of quince, are also in demand; by hardening them in sheets, and then cutting in small squares, sprinkled with white sugar, they may be put up as dry confections, and meet with a ready sale. This class of preserves utilizes all the imperfect fruit, which must otherwise be discarded, as spoiling the effect of the large, handsome specimens that are indispensable when the fruit is to be seen entire; but, when all is mashed together, all that is necessary is to take out any marks of decay, as mutilation does not show.

A lady living in the country on, or near, a fruit farm has great advantages, in the way of preserving, over her city sisters, as the fruit can then be gathered to "taste of the sun," besides costing little or nothing. Transportation of goods, within any reasonable distance, is but a slight additional expense, and a matter very easily managed.

The case of a lady was lately quoted who, with a superabundance of fruit on her premises that could not be disposed of, finally decided to convert it into preserves, and seek a market for it in *that* form. Her experiment has proved eminently successful; and, being fortunate enough to find a home sale for all the preserves she can make, she is now in the receipt of a very handsome income.

Chapter III.

THE HOUSE-KEEPER'S OPPORTUNITIES.
(*Continued.*)

Demand and Supply.—" With *brains*, sir!"—The Pies of Boyhood.—" Money in it."—Advantages of Home-made Pies.—A Waiting Market.—" Apple Pye."—Good Bread.—The Country Baker.—A New Departure.—Modest Beginnings.—Cheap Restaurants.—An Unsupplied Want.—A Bright Idea.—The Ladies' Lunch-room.—Division of Labor.—Coffee at the Sea-shore.—A Money-making Scheme.—Confectionery for Watering-places.

A GOOD house-keeper will be able to make her knowledge remunerative in many ways; and she will soon discover that those who are able to supply a daily recurring want, as in the case of well-prepared food, have no need to seek far for constant employment. People are always wanting things to eat, and eat they will, though other wants may go unsatisfied; hence, those who can cater to this general weakness will succeed where learning and culture fail.

Not that the learning and culture would be amiss even in this very practical calling—for, if Biddy's mistress had Biddy's muscle, she would do the Irish girl's work far better than the Irish girl does it herself; "with *brains*, sir!" being not only an addition, but a manifest improvement, to any combination. A good cook is quite as likely to be found in an accomplished lady as in the red-visaged denizen of the kitchen; and many of those reduced from wealth to comparative poverty have quietly turned their culinary talents to practical account.

Home-made pies and cake, of that ineffable character which men's mothers always made when they were boys, are harder to find than four-leaved clovers; and the success of such exceptional viands is almost assured. There is even a tradition that, some years ago, a woman actually bought a farm with the proceeds of pie-making; but she sold her manufactures herself, and hired no assistants. It is something like those marvellous tales of German farmers on diminutive plots of ground, who contrive to make one acre yield the products of ten—a feat which is accomplished by being their own farmers, hired hands, and errand-boys, and by wasting nothing.

Money can certainly be made, however, by the most retiring lady in manufacturing excellent home-made pies and cake where there is a market for them; and this can be found in any city or town of much size. *Country* housekeepers would feel insulted by the bare suggestion that they were not able and willing to make their own pies and cake, although many of them are not; but dwellers in cities have no such sensitiveness.

Deft fingers with pastry, that can turn out plump, juicy pies of apples in slices, thoroughly cooked, and flavored with cinnamon and orange-peel — those of pumpkin deep, moist, and good in every way, and others in their season—would find no difficulty, after a little patient waiting, perhaps, in meeting with a ready sale for them. People would flock after Mrs. E——'s home-made pies, as they would after Mrs. D——'s home-made preserves; and the agreeable change from strong butter in the paste, and very little of anything in the inside, to crust of flaky sweetness and liberal "filling," could not fail to be appreciated.

Just at first, perhaps, the profit might scarcely pay for the trouble, but a little practice would soon teach the beginner how to buy materials in quantities at a saving, and to use them with discretion. It would not be difficult in the city to find a suitable person to carry the pies around for sale; and there are many business places where they would be warmly welcomed at lunch-time, especially if made in the form of tarts and turnovers. An enterprising lady could do well when her pies became popular; and it is rather surprising that no one has tried the experiment to any extent—that is, no really good, *home-made* pies have been offered for sale in this way; and, because poor ones have not been particularly popular, there is no reason for discouragement where good ones are concerned.

Both pies and cake could probably be introduced into the same market where preserves are welcomed; and, with the help of a competent assistant, a lady could easily supply a large daily demand. She would do well, perhaps, to consider a recipe, not far from two centuries old, called

"APPLE PYE."

"Dear Nelly, learn with Care the Pastry Art,
And mind the easy Precepts I impart;
Draw out your Dough elaborately thin,
And cease not to fatigue your Rolling Pin.
Of Eggs and Butter see you mix enough,
For then the Paste will swell into a Puff,
Which will in crumpling Sounds your Praise report,
And eat, as Housewives speak, exceeding short."

Did any one ever visit a country village where good bread could be bought, or where even *tolerable* bread was offered for sale? The great want of such a place is a decent bakery, where bread worth the eating, biscuits of undoubted character, and good plain cake could be bought. Pies of a like nature might be added here; and, with everything good of its kind, and sufficiently reasonable in price, the projector of such an unusual enterprise could make it an abundantly paying one.

Baker's bread, in the country, is almost invariably dingy of hue and tough of texture; and as to the cakes, or "buns," with their speckled tops, one feels like asking which are currants and which are flies, even at the risk of the traditionary answer, "You pays your *penny*, and you takes your choice." The pies which accompany such bread and cake are not to be thought of, except in the shape of dark mysteries.

In view of this state of things, a depôt, however unpretending, where eatable bread could be had for the buying, with the addition of thoroughly good pies and cake, would surely flourish; and it might begin on a very small scale indeed. A lady's kitchen would furnish all necessary weapons of war, and the services of a person to perform the heaviest labor could be secured by the day, week, or month. A respectable woman could, doubtless, be found to "tend store" for a reasonable consideration; and, when all the wheels of the machinery were fairly in running order, the proprietor would find herself in possession of a substantial business, that must, in the nature of things, prove a lasting one.

As the want is one constantly complained of in country villages—each family being obliged to do its own baking, no matter how inconvenient or unwelcome the task, with the worse alternative of getting their daily supplies from the baker's wagon—a well-managed enterprise of this kind seems to have in it all the elements of success. The little shop might begin in a portion of some one else's store, or even in a room of the dwelling where the highly-respectable "lady attendant" abides; and a moderate trade in confectionery might grow up by degrees under the wing, as it were, of the staff of life. Ice-cream, in warm weather, would also prove remunerative; and there is room, through the length and breadth of the land, for an infinity of these delightful little bakeries, in which ladies can not only make money, but find themselves in the position of public benefactresses.

This is the day of cheap restaurants, where pavement-boys, venders of newspapers, bootblacks, and the like can get a comfortable meal for a few cents; and in far, down-town localities, where business men congregate, a dime or two will procure good meat, bread, milk, tea or coffee, and something quite eatable in the way of dessert.

But for ladies there are no such establishments; the down-town places are too far off, and within a reasonable shopping radius there are only the confectioners, with high prices and unsatisfactory viands. The restaurants established in immense dry goods emporiums in neighboring cities are largely patronized for convenience' sake, and must bring large revenues to their proprietors; but a lady who lately entered one of these apartments, for the purpose of obtaining a much-needed lunch, gives anything but a favorable report of her experience. The crowd had in a measure dispersed, and the new-comer could take her choice of several disorderly-looking tables, with soiled cloths and the crumbs of the last feast. A pert-looking girl came very near to get some ice-cream for another customer, but vouchsafed no reply to the lady's request for a bill of fare; and a colored waiter persistently disregarded her signals.

After five or ten minutes of fruitless waiting, the lady, whose time was precious, rose up in wrath; and, meeting a person who was probably known as the "lady superintendent," she informed her that she was leaving the place because she could get no attention. Everything in the way of attention was immediately promised; but the customer did not find the soiled table-cloths appetizing, and wended her way on her various missions without any lunch at all.

As she walked on, however, decidedly faint and exhausted, she pictured to herself a model lunch-room, intended solely for ladies—the strong point to consist of excellent coffee, supplemented by home-made bread, both white and brown, and the napery and appointments to be immaculate. What a chance, she thought, for some enterprising woman to make a fortune! And why, in the name of common-sense, did not such a woman open just such a restaurant as close as possible to some great shopping centre?

By getting her materials in large quantities, and paying ready money for them, she would find it practicable to charge moderate prices, and yet realize a handsome profit. The mere fact, for instance, of charging five cents a cup for coffee, instead of ten, and yet furnishing an unexceptionable beverage, would bring her a constant run of custom; and the bill of fare could be extended by degrees, as there seemed occasion for it. A small sum of money would go a great way in starting such an establishment, which, at first, could be conducted in one room, with a curtain screen to conceal the little stove, with its coffee apparatus—the bread being made at home; and a respectable, pleasant-spoken woman could be engaged as an attendant.

This would be an experiment on a moderate scale, and the returns would come in daily. The bill of fare could be extended as circumstances required; and, all things considered, the field seems a particularly promising one.

"But," remonstrates Ysolte, helplessly, "what has this to do with *me?* I am not a house-keeper, and cannot set up a restaurant."

Then she can go into partnership with some friend who *is* a house-keeper; or, if she has no available friend, she can probably find, by careful search, some worthy woman who will be only too glad to do her cooking for a fair consideration; while the other worthy woman who presides over the lunch-room can easily manage the coffee. The few articles needed at first can be collected very cheaply; and, if situated in the right neighborhood, there will be no lack of custom.

There is a want yet to be supplied at sea-shore places of resort, and a want, too, that, strangely enough, seems to have entirely escaped the notice of those who prey upon the seekers after health and pleasure. This is the cup of fragrant coffee that always follows the Turkish bath, but which has as yet had no connection with a plunge into the ocean.

An excellent opportunity for money-making here offers itself to any one who is capable of carrying out such an enterprise. Few bathers would not be willing to pay ten cents for the refreshment of an excellent cup of coffee at the very time when it is most wanted; and its reviving effects are particularly noticeable after the fatigues of bathing and getting dressed again.

The coffee could be served in some place close at hand, or it might be carried around on waiters; but it should invariably be hot and strong, and able to bear the closest criticism. A woman to make the coffee, with an assistant to help her pour it out, and boys or girls to carry it around, would constitute the needed corps; while the proprietor might disport herself among the bathers, and even partake of a cup of her own coffee, if she felt so inclined.

Confectionery is always a popular article of merchandize at watering-places; and anything a little out of the common way, if good as well, would be received with favor. Whether bought or home-made, if nicely put up in boxes of a convenient size and sold at a reasonable price, the demand for it would be quite extensive.

An arrangement might be made with the hotel-keeper, or with some one living in the place, to undertake the sale; but ordinary ingenuity will furnish methods for accomplishing this according to the circumstances of the case.

Chapter IV.

WHAT MAY BE DONE WITH THE NEEDLE.

Use and Abuse of the Needle.—Ladies' Depositories.—A Museum of Fancy-work.—Judgment and Invention.—Society of Decorative Art.—Quaint Productions.—Profitable but Unattractive Work.—Indian Bead-work.—An Old Woman's Emery-bags.—A Monopoly Desirable.—Small Inventions.—Knitting and Crocheting.—Dress-making and Millinery.—Convenience and Economy.—Travelling Advantages.—Pins *vs.* Needles.—Home Dress-making.—An Easy Way of Learning.—Private Remunerative Work.—A Lady's Experiment.—Observation and Ingenuity.—A Neglected Art.—An Establishment for Repairs.

A DEFT use of the needle is a particularly lady-like accomplishment; but plain sewing is hard and wearing work, and, since the introduction of sewing-machines, it is, when "done by hand," anything but remunerative. As an essentially feminine implement, the needle

THE NEEDLE. 61

had always been a great favorite with poets and writers, until the "Song of the Shirt" opened their eyes to the evils caused by an excessive use of it; and scarcely a more affecting picture can be drawn than that of a poor, half-starved needle-woman bending over her daily toil.

In all the large cities there are emporiums, generally known as Ladies' Depositories, where ladies (for whose benefit they are intended) can deposit articles of needle-work made by them for sale, receiving the proceeds when sold, after the deduction of the usual ten per cent. commission; while ladies who want work done deposit it there to be given out to the proper persons. All kinds of plain sewing and embroidery are done through these establishments; but only first-class work is accepted, as the prices paid are very liberal.

These institutions have proved perfect boons to many poor, proud ones, who could not bring themselves openly to join the ranks of sewing-women, and yet whose only power lay in a skilful use of the needle. A perfect museum of fancy-work, beautifully executed, and often showing taste and originality in the combinations, is displayed in windows and cases; and it is saddening to see such an' apparently inexhaustible supply of pin-cushions, and tidies, and babies' socks, and afghans, and every fanciful allurement that can be thought of to open the purses of wealthy visitors, because there are so few purchasers in proportion to the supply.

The best season for the sale of such articles is during the month before the Christmas holidays, when an inventive fancy and dexterous fingers may be turned to good account. The surest element of success is to produce something that is original, and at the same time in demand; and inexpensive trifles will sell much more readily than elaborate pieces of work.

The Society of Decorative Art is very much the same thing on a higher scale, hand-painting and artistic embroidery being the only accomplishments that find admission there. Very beautiful work is displayed, and high prices are paid to those who come up to the standard required; but, to do this, careful study is necessary, and considerable outlay both of time and money.

Ordinarily, the sale of fancy-work depends upon the place and the season as much as upon the workmanship. In some quaint, sea-shore places shell-work, which in cities is thought too antiquated to be worthy of notice, is largely in demand; and in one sandy retreat, not unknown to fame, a maiden lady partly supports herself by her "shell pieces." These are composed of small shells and fragments of coral, dotted over a mass of sea-weed that issues from a diminutive basket, or, rather, from the flat half of it—all of which is glued on a foundation of card-board, ready for the frame, which is added by the purchaser.

Numbers of these works of art are carried away as mementos of the place; and some of them are really pretty. The handsomest ones, in which a flat pearl shell of lovely, changeful sheen is substituted for the basket, are sold for several dollars apiece. A peep, however, into the work-room, back of the shop, where the shell-artist stains her hands with powerful acids that are used to bring out the beauty of the shells, is not calculated to attract fastidious ladies to this occupation.

Indian bead-work has its attractions when bought of Indians, and some ladies manufacture it on a very elaborate scale for fancy fairs; but what could a city shopkeeper do with it? Who would care for the crosses and trinkets made of table-rock away from Niagara?

Some years ago a poor old woman, whose eyesight was exceptionally good, helped to support herself and a family of grandchildren by making emery-bags. The strawberries, both white and red, with their clearly-defined green hulls, were wonderfully natural-looking, some being made of flannel, and some of velvet, and varying in price, according to the material; and a ready sale was found for these useful little articles among the ladies who took an interest in the aged needle-woman. The materials, fortunately, cost her nothing—bits of flannel, velvet, and silk being furnished by the ladies themselves; while the emery, which was of the very best quality, was the gift of a dealer in such goods.

Almost any one small article for which there is a demand, and especially one of which the manufacturer, as inventor also, has the monopoly, will bring in better returns than a variety of articles of less decided popularity. One reason for this can probably be found in the fact that, when the powers are concentrated on the doing of one thing only, that thing is sure to be done exceptionally well.

Any invention that pleases children is an *open sesame* to their parents' purses; and a quick-witted young lady has netted herself into quite a profitable little business by making hammocks for dolls. These little hammocks are made both of silk and cotton, of prettily contrasting colors, and finished with dainty bows of ribbon where they are suspended. To have one's beloved Florence Arabella gently swaying to and fro (a miniature edition of Sister Lil, who, with æsthetic attire and the last novel, is doing the same thing in a shaded corner of the veranda) in a hammock of her own is infinitely delicious to the juvenile mind; and it is easy to believe that such an article, as the advertisers say, "sells at sight."

Some ladies knit and crochet with such dexterity that their work is much in demand; and, although the stores pay very poorly for this kind of labor, private orders are often received through friends that make it worth the doing. One or two hundred dollars a year can be very pleasantly earned by working with soft, bright wools, and making pretty articles in one's leisure hours. There is, however, no regular demand for this kind of manufactures, and such orders are usually the result of good fortune and influence—fancy-work of any kind being a very poor staff to lean upon.

Dress-making and millinery, which, if such a term is allowable, may be called fancy plain sewing, are particularly satisfactory in their results.

There is a very general belief that dress-makers and milliners are born, instead of being made; and this idea is verified by the ease with which some persons, without the least instruction, will take up the making of dresses or bonnets, and turn out work that would be creditable to those regularly apprenticed to the trade. When only put to home uses the gift is a most convenient one, and a saving both of trouble and money; for good dressmakers, at reasonable prices, are as rare as good servants, and good milliners equally so.

If there is truth in the homely adage that a penny saved is a penny gained, economy may be considered in the light of money-making; and that there is a great saving in the making of one's own dresses and bonnets is an undisputed fact. Less material is required; things can be made to "do," in the way of linings and trimmings, that would be most contemptuously regarded by a professional lady, and a delightful feeling of independence is attained by having one's dress-maker and milliner always at hand for repairs and alterations.

The convenience of this in travelling, or while on a visit, can scarcely be exaggerated; and, in packing things into a small compass, the lady who does her own millinery can indulge in three or four hats, where her more helpless sister could allow herself but one. To effect this, the hats are entirely stripped of trimming—the feathers, flowers, ribbons, etc., carefully laid in the tray or box prepared for them—while the denuded skeletons are placed one within another, as at the hatters, and stowed with the smallest amount of attention or respect just where they will go conveniently.

It is an assured fact that one phase of the unpacking consists in reclothing these naked hats—a thing that is easily done with the help of a few pins, a twist or two, and a stitch here and there. Amateur milliners advocate the use of pins rather than of needles; but professionals may not endorse this theory.

The dress-maker, too, can divest her handiwork of any trimming or draping that might be injured by close packing, secure in the power of being able to restore each flounce and fold to its original place, as soon as the time has come for the garment to emerge from its chrysalis state.

In a family of several daughters, even where there is a reasonable supply of money, an aptness for dress-making and millinery is a gift to be cultivated. One *paterfamilias* offered his eldest daughter a new dress for every dress of similar value that she made satisfactorily for herself, or for any other member of the family; and the young lady applied herself so diligently to the art, that her wardrobe was the wonder and admiration of all her friends.

When it is a possible thing for a lady to acquire this useful knowledge, she should not hesitate to do so; and some good dress-makers and milliners are now willing to receive pupils in place of apprentices. If regular instruction is not available, a great deal may be learned by taking an old dress or bonnet to pieces, to see how it is put together; and this, with the aid of the excellent patterns that are sold everywhere, would enable almost any one to achieve a fair degree of success.

Any lady with some degree of taste in this branch of needle-work will be able to make it profitable in a moderate way among her friends, who will be glad enough to secure work worthy, perhaps, of a first-class *modiste* at not more than half her charges. The workers, on the other hand, feel that they are well remunerated, and are thankful to obtain new bonnets and dresses for themselves by fashioning those of their friends.

The millinery business is said to be extremely profitable; and two ladies, who were desirous of obtaining money for a certain purpose, were once engaged in it for a year in a somewhat novel way.

One partner had all the artistic taste, and made the bonnets, which were charming; the other was of a practical, business turn, and attended to the purchases and the account-keeping. A room was hired in a desirable locality, and a trustworthy saleswoman placed in it; while the real proprietors were never supposed to be connected with the establishment at all.

These enterprising ladies realized a handsome profit, and retired at the end of a year with their purpose fully accomplished.

A milliner in a country village is sure to become well-to-do, at least; and one with taste and a knowledge of business might do much better than this. Quick powers of observation are necessary to success, as well as the ability to originate styles, and to combine and arrange trimmings effectively. A man-milliner complained that he walked out on the most public thoroughfare for the express purpose of studying the different styles, but that none of the women whom he employed as assistants ever did so.

Some persons can almost in a single glance make a novelty their own; and these are born milliners and dress-makers. Others can gaze for a few moments in a window, and then come home and cut their own patterns, giving just the right look to every part. Such women need never be in want—they carry a fortune in their quick eyes and nimble fingers.

That branch of needle-work known as *mending* is often sadly neglected, and the exquisitely regular, back-and-forth darning of a past generation usually excites comments on the " waste " of the time bestowed upon it. Some things are worth mending and others are not; but, as a general rule, if a thing is worth mending at all, it is worth mending well.

To understand mending thoroughly is a great aid to economy; and the patch put on by a thread, and sewed with almost invisible stitches, often saves a valuable garment, without materially affecting its appearance. To regard mending, however, in the light of a money-making industry is so much of a novelty, that the following paragraph from a daily paper will be read with interest:

"It is somewhat singular that, among the many devices resorted to by women for the purpose of earning a livelihood, it has not yet dawned upon the consciousness of some enterprising females that general repair establishments could be made grand successes in large cities. Just where the thousands of young men who are away from their mothers, sisters, or aunts get their mending done is a mystery. That it is done by somebody, there is no doubt; but, if there were places where a shirt, a pair of stockings, drawers, pantaloons, or any other garment could be sent to be mended, with the assurance that it would be neatly and cheaply done, there would be no lack of patronage. Many families would avail themselves of such facilities, for there is no duty incumbent upon the female head of the house more generally distasteful than that of repairing clothing.

"We throw out these suggestions for the benefit of whom they may concern. There are many splendid openings for such repair shops in ——; and the enterprising woman who opens the first one will be well rewarded, if she does it in a proper way."

Chapter V.

TEACHING IN ITS VARIOUS BRANCHES.

The Profession of Teaching.—"Classes and Lessons."—Ordinary Remuneration.—A Class in Literature.—A Few Suggestions.—The Study of Botany.—Reading Aloud.—Ordinary Failings.—Reading to an Invalid.—Music Lessons.—A Modern Cecilia.—Appreciation.—Instruction in Fancy-work.—A Sewing-school.—A Class in Mending.—An Object to Work for.—Cooking-schools.—Teaching as an Exchange.

HAVING considered the various branches which come under the heads of house-keeping and needle-work, there now remains for discussion the profession of teaching, as the last of the three legitimate occupations for *ladies* in what might be called the Dark Ages of women's work.

Teaching, in spite of its care and anxiety and wearying, tread-mill round of duties, has always been a popular employment with the educated—principally because it is one of the few means of money-making in which a lady may openly engage without compromising her social standing.

There are many who, without being able to give *all* their time to teaching, would gladly be so engaged for two or three days of the week, or two or three hours of each day; and "classes" and "lessons" have multiplied so of late years that a qualified instructor seldom experiences any difficulty in carrying out such a plan. In a large city there are often to be found fully-grown, and even middle-aged, people desirous of instruction, because of a lack of early advantages; and a lady with influential recommendations—and even without them, through some happy accident—can usually find occupation among this class for an hour or two of the day.

The price for such instruction varies from fifty cents to a dollar an hour, even exceeding this in some cases; and a well-worded advertisement in a daily journal will seldom fail to bring pupils to the would-be teachers. The pupils themselves sometimes advertise for teachers; and it is the custom to furnish responsible references on both sides.

A class in literature is a delightful employment for those who are qualified to engage in it, and one that is always well remunerated. In the cities such positions are apt to be filled to overflowing; but in small towns and country places opportunities of this kind are not so numerous. It would not be difficult, within a distance, perhaps, of two or three miles, to collect a class of young girls who would be glad to avail themselves of the services of a lady competent to direct their reading, and introduce them into the higher walks of literature.

A class which met twice a week, paying fifty cents each for a lesson, would yield a very nice weekly sum for the amount of time given, and would also be a very pleasant means of increasing one's spending-money. Those who feel distrustful of their own powers in an attempt to guide others would find some useful hints in a small volume called "A Course of English Reading." This contains many valuable suggestions in regard to particular lines of reading and study that could be turned to good account by any one beginning a class in literature.

The study of botany, which might be conducted in quite an original manner by reading in connection what old poets and new have written on the subject of flowers, could thus be made particularly attractive, involving picnics and various excursions, with charming collections for gardens and vases.

With a teacher capable of making things as interesting as they *could* be made, such classes would be found eminently successful even in the smallest place; and many unappropriated fields are ready for the experiment.

The advantages of good reading—reading aloud for the pleasure of others—are beginning to be appreciated; and a properly qualified teacher, not of "elocution"—which always suggests making up faces and speaking a piece—but of easy, unconstrained reading aloud, would seldom fail to obtain sufficient encouragement. So many books are now to be had on the proper management of the voice, that almost any lady, with ordinarily good vocal powers, could soon remedy the defects in her own reading, and make herself competent to instruct others.

Reading aloud is too often performed in a high-pitched, unnatural tone, with as little regard to final *d's* and *g's* as prevails among other speakers of the English tongue in their dealings with the letter *h*. These faults once overcome, a natural, conversational style is not difficult to acquire; and reading-classes, with a fair and good-natured contest at the end of a term for a prize to the best reader, could be made quite popular in the list of village enjoyments in winter.

Occasionally, a good reader will be able to find a couple of hours' daily employment in reading aloud to an invalid, or one whose eyes will not bear use; but such opportunities are not of frequent occurrence, being in many cases only a delicate *ruse* on the part of the wealthy to put money into the hand of a poor but proud friend. Such an engagement, however, can sometimes be made even with strangers, and there are few more agreeable ways of earning a regular salary.

Giving music lessons "just for pin-money" is a very general practice, and the music teacher, especially when the pupils are small children, in a country village, frequently appears in the shape of a young lady very much dressed. The employment is very remunerative under a reasonable amount of patronage; and the hard-working mechanic and his equally hard-working wife are particularly anxious to have their daughters taught to "play the pianner." To see Celia or "Hanner Jane" seated, of a morning, at the instrument, in "unwomanly rags" and unkempt hair, shrieking forth the pathetic complaint—

"No one to love me,
None to caress,"

far from producing acquiescence in the justice of such a fate, excites a pleasant thrill of satisfaction in the parental bosoms that this gifted being is actual household property.

The thoroughly trained and competent music-teacher will find more congenial pupils, and receive a liberal price for her lessons. A little extra income earned in this way often enables the teacher to improve herself in the higher branches of her art; and when the pupils are friends, or children of friends, the occupation can be made a very pleasant one.

A class in fancy-work would be found very taking in small places, where such advantages are not so easily obtained as in the city; and the ruling mania, whatever it might be, would be eagerly sought after. The old-fashioned mania for wax flowers was revived some years ago, and teachers of the art found it very profitable; but it is decidedly out of favor now, except in remote places. One dollar an hour is the usual price for such instruction; or it may be given, like embroidery in silk, gold bullion, etc., in a course of so many lessons. Stitches in knitting, crochet-work, and ordinary embroidery do not command so high a price.

Instruction in plain needle-work is much needed, and not so easy to obtain as instruction in fancy-work. Quite lately, in a small country place, a lady opened a sewing-school on Saturdays, which was well attended by girls from twelve to fifteen. Only plain sewing and mending were taught—accomplishments usually more appreciated by parents than by pupils; but the attendance of the volatile damsels was secured by an interesting story read aloud during the lessons, and some little refreshment and a game of romps at the end. The two hours' instruction was well remunerated; and there are few mothers, able to do so, who would not gladly pay for having their girls thoroughly grounded in the rudiments of needlework by one who understands the art, and who also understands half-grown girls.

A mending-class would be a novelty, but, in connection with plain sewing, it could scarcely fail of success. There are always stockings to darn, and ravages to repair, in the best-regulated families; but there is not always some one who can do these things properly, and sometimes the repairing is worse than the rent. The woman who can mend well has all that is saved in this way added to her income; and few more profitable and convenient uses can be found for needle and thread.

Such a class could be made very interesting by having an object to work for. Each pupil might bring the discarded garments of the family to be repaired for the use of the poor, or placed, when good enough, in a box for foreign or domestic missions; for, with such an incentive, unsuspected talent, in the way of making old clothes look almost as good as new, would be developed to a surprising extent.

Cooking-schools are not a modern device in the way of teaching, but an old one revived. It used to be the fashion to teach ladies how to cook; but this instruction probably took the form of wonderful cakes and confections, rather than that of ordinary viands

> ". . . Not too good
> For human nature's daily food."

A school similar to those now established in two or three large cities, teaching thoroughly the preparation of common family meals, would be appreciated in most towns and settlements; and a lady known by her neighbors to be an adept in making bread, biscuits, and cakes, need not often seek for pupils in vain. The arts of pickling, preserving, sirup and wine making, might be added; and the graduates of such a school could give an entertainment provided by their own fair hands, each dish being labelled with the name of the maker.

Almost any gift may be turned to account in the way of teaching, provided it is something that one's neighbors care to learn; and sometimes an exchange may be made, without the medium of currency, that will prove of mutual advantage. A person, for instance, well supplied with fruit, vegetables, or the like, may be glad to part with a portion of these commodities in payment for instruction; while the other party is equally glad to receive so useful an equivalent for the money earned. Both are thus accommodated; but, if a money return had been insisted on, no arrangement could have been effected between them.

Other forms of instruction may be suggested by these brief hints, which are not intended for those who are able to devote the whole of their time to the business of teaching.

Chapter VI.

LITERATURE AND WRITING.

"Prose and Worse."—Undeveloped Talent.—Mistaken Ideas.—Some Open Doors.—A Mercenary View of the Subject.—What to Write About.—Rates of Remuneration.—Literary Giants.—Century Plants.—What an Author Needs.—Novel Writing a Trade.—Works of Fiction.—Profits of Periodical Literature.—Elements of Success.—Value of Advertising.—Sensational Writers.—A Lady's Attempt with a Dime Novel.—Sunday-school Books.—A List of Periodicals.—Writing by Proxy.—Advertisements.—Letter-writing.—Legal Copying.—Book-keeping.

WITHIN the last few years, when so many non-toilers have been compelled to consider more or less the subject of money-making, the discovery has been very generally made that literary work is the most agreeable and remunerative of the various occupations suitable for a lady.

This general conviction has inundated the market with attempts in "prose and worse;" while bitter disappointment awaited the owners of bulky manuscripts who imagined writing to be "the easiest thing in the world to do."

A poet says that

"Men have been cradled into poetry by wrong,"

and it is well known that circumstances often bring to light unsuspected talent —a poem, or a novel, of undisputed merit, having sometimes been written to meet a financial crisis; but such cases are rare, and triumphs of this kind are almost invariably preceded by underground work of *some* sort.

That a person of good average education, who needs money badly, can, with a little practice, make literature a means of support, is a very pleasing fallacy, but one that has very little foundation in fact.

The ability merely to write acceptably and profitably is very delightful, but it does not come all at once; and to many, who are ambitious of it, it never comes at all. Culture and the advantages of society are valuable aids in the development of literary talent, but they cannot bestow it where it does not exist, and much, on the other hand, may be done without them.

A pretty poem, a graceful story, or a bright little volume, may be within the reach of those by whom the higher triumphs of literature are never attained; and all these things have usually a decided market value. There are so many different kinds of writing — so many channels opened in magazine and newspaper literature, and especially in books and stories for children—that there is a niche for almost everything that is really good. So little outlay, too, is required

—pen, ink, and paper, and a few postage-stamps constituting the capital—that the least chance of success seems to justify the beginner in making the attempt.

In these pages writing is viewed, like every other employment, solely in regard to its money returns: of the higher aims of genius, and a conscientious desire to benefit mankind, it is out of place to speak here. For those who need such information, the following paragraphs, from a work on women's employments, published some time ago, may be found useful:

"Subjects," says the writer, "are as numerous as the objects around us, and suited to all moods and diversities of mind. To the contributor I would say: Your writing will be likely to find readers, whether it be grave or gay, sad or sprightly, witty or jovial; whether one making a draught on the imagination or the judgment; whether one displaying your own attainments, or calling to aid the opinions and requirements of others; in short, one of thought, fancy, or facts.

"Your friends may like your ideas draped in poetry, or the more substantial dress of prose. One is like gold, the other like iron. One serves for ornament, the other for use. The true poet is a gifted person—a heaven-born talent does he or she possess. If you have good descriptive talents, you can write stories— laying the scenes in far-away countries that are not much known, and yet eliciting some interest. And as to the subjects of a moral cast, their name is legion. Magazine-writing furnishes a palatable way of drawing attention to individual follies, or furnishing a satire on the inconsistencies and exactions of society in general. If you attempt to write natural stories, let your scenes and events be such as occur in every-day life."

As to the prices paid for acceptable articles, they vary according to the style of the article and the character of the periodical, as well as the reputation of the writer. Harpers' periodicals pay about ten dollars for a thousand words; the *Atlantic Monthly* about the same price per page; and others in proportion to their circulation and cost. Some of the little Sunday-school papers, which require tiny articles, make very tiny returns. A lady lately received from one of them a very polite note containing a dollar bill, and stating that it was "in payment for her 'Camelopard'"— a fragment of natural history which, fortunately for her, she had not valued very highly.

The paper in question is an honest, substantial little sheet, that always pays for what it uses at a settled rate per column; but there are periodicals whose proprietors will publish articles, even by well-known writers, and then calmly say that "it is not their custom to pay for contributions unless arrangements to that effect are made beforehand!" It is safer, therefore, except in writing for the periodicals mentioned, and those of similar standing, to make the arrangements beforehand.

In an article written some time ago it is said: "I have now before me a statement from a single publisher, in which he says that to Messrs. Willis, Longfellow, Bryant, and Allston his price was uniformly $50 for a poetical article, long or short; and his readers know that they were generally very short—in one case, only fourteen lines. To numerous others it was from $25 to $40. In one case he has paid $25 a page for prose. To Mr.

Cooper he paid $1800 for a novel, and $1000 for a series of naval biographies, the author retaining the copyright for separate publication; and in such cases, if the work be good, its appearance in the magazine acts as the best of advertisements. To Mr. James he paid $1200 for a novel, leaving him also the copyright. For a single number of his journal he has paid to authors $1500.

These names, most of which belong to the literature of a past generation, show that the article is by no means a modern one; and at the present day there are women-writers who receive even greater sums than these. Mrs. Stowe, Mrs. Hodgson-Burnett, and Miss Phelps are probably the best paid of our female authors; but these ladies have exceptional talent, and belong rather to the century-plant order.

Their humble sisters, however, need

not despair of a moderate degree of success; and those who fancy that they possess any powers of imagination and expression have at least the right to try their wings. "The indispensable qualifications to make a writer are—a talent for literary composition, an accurate knowledge of language, and an acquaintance with the subject to be treated."

Mr. Anthony Trollope declared that novel-writing could be made as much a matter of apprenticeship as any other trade; and he carried out his views by bringing up his son to his own calling. The volumes thus produced by machinery are not remarkable for freshness; but they show what may be done by regularly learning the trade.

In works of fiction there is always a wide field for women. "This class of books requires less time, less study, and less money, and rewards the authors pecuniarily better, than any other kind of work, considering, of course, the comparatively small amount of application required." This is the universal testimony; and a poor story is often more salable than an admirably written, instructive article devoid of entertainment.

People write from many different motives, such as love of fame, wealth, influence, and a desire to do good; if from the second motive, there are various things to be considered. Among these is the testimony of a very successful writer that she made a mistake in devoting most of her time to periodical literature, as books are infinitely more profitable; and Rose Terry Cooke, one of our most charming magazinists, whose stories are probably quarrelled for by the editors, instead of ever being returned to her, distinctly states that she has never yet made by her pen one thousand dollars a year. Had she produced a book, her account would probably have been very different.

The most *immediately* remunerative kind of book is a bright, taking story that can be read of a summer's day—a book with a title that seizes the fancy at once, and in which commonplace occurrences are treated in an uncommon way. Originality of expression is a powerful ingredient to success; and delicate touches of this kind are most effective in completing an attractive whole. Who does not remember that, among the many charms of "Rutledge," the heroine had no name?

Literary merit, although indispensable to an enduring fame, is by no means necessary to moneyed success; and a recent review of a popular volume gives a fair idea of what is needed:

"The reason of the great success of

—————— lies almost wholly outside its covers; it is not due to anything for which the author is to be held responsible at all, excepting the title. Given at any time a catching title, enough merit to rescue the volume from dulness, and an abundance of ingenious advertising, and what trifle of the kind could not be forced into large circulation? There must, however, be comparatively a taking phrase in the title, as well as extensive placarding, to secure the result; divorce one from the other, and a different story would be the consequence."

Sensational periodicals and papers, that deal in blood-and-thunder literature, pay poorly for the work done, but require large supplies of it. Occasionally, some modern Scherezade, who can spin a story out endlessly, and season it highly with blood-curdling adventures, receives a handsome salary for her weekly contributions. One of this class of writers had the first story sent to a certain paper returned to her, "to be rewritten grammatically and spelled correctly"—English and orthography being equally abominable; but madam responded that "she couldn't write at all, if she had to bother about the grammar and spelling." The quick eye of the reader had detected in the untidy sheets a decided genius for hair-breadth escapes, and midnight murders, and mysterious poisonings; and as these uncanny subjects formed the staple of his programme, he hired a person to decipher the manuscripts and reduce them to a civilized condition, while the gifted authoress was placed on the regular staff at an absurdly high rate of remuneration.

It is scarcely possible for an educated and refined lady to do this kind of writing successfully. One who attempted it some years ago often refers to it as an amusing experience. She had been advised to write a dime novel, which was represented as a very easy task, and sure to bring in a certain moderate sum—the great point being to make it as sensational as possible. For a first attempt in this style, our authoress felt that she had acquitted herself very creditably in making her hero, in the first chapter, go crazy, and all but commit suicide, kill his child, and turn his wife out-of-doors; but the manuscript was returned to her, with a polite note, stating that *it was of too domestic a character to answer their purpose!*

Having done her very worst, the lady retired from the field discomfited.

Sunday-school books of the right kind are very much needed — not religious novels, but books suitable for intelligent children from ten to fifteen years of age.

It is probably owing to the prevalent idea that a Sunday-school book is very easy to write, that the market is flooded with such a quantity of trash; but a book of this kind, that shall accomplish its high mission, cannot be written by every one.

There is no dearth of subjects; there are such beautiful things in Nature to those who have learned to look up to Nature's God, such a wealth of clouds and sunsets and early dawns, with all the witching changes of the seasons; and, far more beautiful even than these, the lovely, heroic deeds of daily life that sometimes gild the humblest homes, and wind like a thread of gold through the most prosaic and unpromising surroundings. Such materials are always at hand for the true artist.

Commonplace, goody-goody books—narratives that are largely composed of conversations in which the characters "grind" in a style that would not be tolerated in real life — have had their day. The author of a volume of this description rather boasted that, when she began to write, she had not the slightest idea what she was going to say. "That is just what I should have supposed from reading it," replied her plain-spoken auditor.

The power that is needed in Sunday-school literature is the ability to take the common, every-day events of ordinary life and make of them sermons that shall elevate and encourage all who read them:

> "Footprints that perchance another,
>   Sailing o'er life's rugged main,
>   Some forlorn and shipwrecked brother,
>   Seeing, shall take heart again."

A list of the various periodicals which pay for contributions, some liberally, and others very moderately, may be of use to those who are just beginning to write for publication. Those marked with a star are children's periodicals:

Harper's Magazine	New York.
" Weekly	" "
" Bazar	" "
" Young People*.	" "
Scribner's Monthly	" "
St. Nicholas*.	" "
Leslie's Lady's Journal	" "
" Sunday Magazine	" "
" Chimney Corner	" "
Demorest's Monthly	" "
Magazine of American History	" "
The Churchman	" "
The Independent	" "
The Christian Weekly	" "
The Christian Union	" "
The Home Journal	" "
The Daily Graphic	" "
Lippincott's Magazine	Philadelphia.
Arthur's Home Magazine	"
Godey's Lady's Book	"
Peterson's Magazine	"
The Sunday-school Times	"
The Youth's World*	"

The Sabbath-school Visitor*	Philadelphia.
The Atlantic Monthly	Boston.
The Youth's Companion*	"
Ballou's Monthly	"
The Waverley Magazine	"
Wide Awake*	"
The Congregationalist	"
The Wellspring*	"
The Dayspring*	"

There are probably others scattered over the country; but those enumerated will be more than sufficient for the most industrious writer.

Sometimes persons with a ready pen, but not much literary genius, make a good income by doing other people's writing; and lectures that are delivered with considerable effect are not always the work of the speaker. A case was lately mentioned of a young man who earned a comfortable living by writing lectures, pamphlets for patent medicines, and advertisements.

An enterprising woman, too, was cited who first secured an entire column in a daily paper—which she obtained at a greatly reduced rate from that charged for single advertisements; then she visited different business people—or sent persons whom she employed for that purpose—representing to them the great advantages of advertising in that particular column; and, finally, she wrote out the advertisements in an attractive style and had them inserted, very much to her own advantage.

Writing letters for those who are not gifted in expressing themselves has occasionally been found profitable; and persons with a very large correspondence are often glad to avail themselves of such help. The duties of an amanuensis are comparatively light, and the remuneration fair.

But copying for lawyers, for which

there are so many advertisements in the daily papers, is by no means a desirable employment. It is represented as very dirty, tiresome work, and poorly paid. Three cents for every hundred words is an exceptional rate, as it is oftener less; a very clear, round, legible handwriting is required, and any mistake must be rectified by doing the work over. On the whole, there are many employments more attractive than this.

Directing envelopes is very much of the same nature; and a small sum is paid for them by the thousand. Sometimes these employments can be carried on in one's own house; but oftener they are regular office-work, and quite out of the question for a lady.

Chapter VII.

ART INDUSTRIES.

Schools of Design.—Fundamental Instruction.—Impossible Achievements.—Practical Skill in Designing.—Mechanical Drawing.—Women as Architects.—Engraving on Gold and Silver.—The New York Society of Decorative Art.—Objects of the Society.—A Depot for First-class Work.—Conditions for Exhibitors.—China Painting.—The Decoration of Fans.—Hand-screens, Plaques, etc.—Door-panels.—Illustrations for Books.—A Superfluity of Genius.

The Schools of Design which have been opened in most of the large cities afford ladies many advantages for learning how to make money pleasantly. The course is rather tiresome, perhaps, for a grown person, and especially for one feeling the need of speedy returns for any investment, even of time—four years being the time required for graduation; but, if a pupil desires to study some particular branch for a limited period, arrangements can generally be made to do so.

The peculiar advantages offered by the School of Design are the very thorough nature of the instruction, the abundance and variety of models to work from, and the very moderate charges to those who intend making it in any way a means of support. The industrial branches of the fine arts receive especial attention; and the opportunities for acquiring a practical knowledge of designing, lithography, wood-engraving, etc., in addition to all kinds of drawing and painting, are quite unrivalled.

It has been said that the greater part of the higher order of designs are practically unavailable for want of knowledge on the part of the designer of the conditions of the particular manufacture in question. The economic possibility and aptitude are not studied; and hence, the manufacturers say, are enormous wastes of thought, skill, and industry. This want supplied, a field of industry practically boundless would be opened to female artists, as well as artisans; and it would be an enlightened policy to look to this, while the whole world seems to be opening its ports to our productions.

These considerations make the popular stories of heroines who achieve, without any preliminary training, the highest success in their first attempts at designing utter absurdities—the most unpretentious of wall-paper patterns requiring some idea of means to an end to make it available. Such employments are delightful enough in themselves to repay a reasonable amount of application to the study of rudiments; and a well-grounded designer, with an inventive fancy, will find abundant and well-remunerated work.

Practical skill in drawing is absolutely essential to a good designer; and, with this foundation, the study becomes an easy one. Wall-papers and calicoes consume endless designs; and, in addition, there are carpets, silks, ribbons, furniture, lace, silver, jewellery, etc.

Many ladies make quite a handsome income by drawing for the Patent Office, patent agents, etc., the drawings being chiefly linear, mechanical ones, and the remuneration varying according to ability. The fact, however, is emphasized that "it requires mechanical knowledge, which is not very often possessed by women, but is a branch of study that would be found both pleasant and profitable, especially if they were prepared for it by an elementary course in the public schools. It is not a branch that admits of much display, and is, therefore, almost entirely neglected, or taught in such a way as to be utterly futile for all practical purposes."

Architectural drawing is also a useful, pleasant, and *very* profitable acquirement; and there is no reason why women should not be eminently successful as architects. Houses planned by ladies could scarcely fail to be more satisfactory in detail, and very much more convenient; and some especially comfortable and attractive houses have been so planned. It is quite an unusual thing to see a lady pursuing the study or practice of architecture; and yet "the wife of Erwin von Steinbach materially assisted her husband in the erection of the famous Strasbourg Cathedral; and within its walls a sculptured stone represents the husband and wife as consulting together on the plan."

Almost every woman sees something to change in the house she inhabits, and knows just how *she* would have ordered the arrangement of closets, staircases, etc., to economize room to the best advantage; but, without some knowledge of the rudiments of architecture, it is not easy to draw a plan that can be practically carried out. A proper course of instruction, combined with the natural inclination of women for comforts and conveniences in the place where so much of their lives is spent, would result in a new and improved order of house architecture, as well as remunerative and lady-like employment to many who are now wondering what they can do.

Engraving of various kinds is a popular branch of study at the School of Design—a knowledge of this art insuring constant and remunerative employment.

The work of ladies in chasing on gold and silver is frequently in demand; and the qualifications needed are good drawing and penmanship.

While the instructions received in the School of Design are more particularly directed to the industrial branches of the fine arts, the Societies of Decorative Art furnish a somewhat higher and more æsthetic culture. China-painting, tile-painting, panel-painting, art needle-work, and everything of an ornamental nature that conforms to the principles of true art, receive careful attention; and a market is provided for all work that may be found satisfactory.

The instruction in these institutions is not free, except for a limited number of pupils who may have sufficiently influential friends to procure scholarships for them; but the salesrooms offer unusual advantages in disposing of all work that is approved by the Committees.

The New York Society of Decorative Art states the objects of its institution to be:

"1st. To establish a place for the exhibition and sale of decorative work, and to encourage the production of such work among women.

"2d. To distribute information with regard to the various art industries which have been found profitable in other countries, and to increase the supply of hand-wrought decoration.

"3d. To induce art-workers to master thoroughly the details of some one method of decoration, not only that they may make for themselves a reputation of commercial value, but that they may also assist in establishing a high standard of excellence.

"4th. To assist those who have worked unsuccessfully in choosing some practical and popular direction for their labor.

"5th. To form classes in various kinds of decorative work.

"6th. To establish a library of books and manuals of design.

"7th. To form connections with manufacturers and importers, and to obtain orders from private individuals, and from dealers in decorated pottery, china, tiles, cabinet-work, carvings, draperies, embroideries, and articles of household art.

"8th. To develop the beautiful art of needle-work, and assist in adapting it to the requirements of house-furnishing and decoration.

"9th. To furnish a market, outside of a limited circle of friends, for the large amount of artistic work done by those who do not make it a profession, but who have attained a professional skill in execution."

The last clause is of especial interest to those for whom these pages are intended; and a number of ladies gifted with artistic taste and skilful fingers find the society rooms a most satisfactory depot for their productions. A visit to these rooms is an introduction to the principles of ornamental art; and only objects of dainty design and finished execution are admitted to the artistically arranged shelves and tables.

Here may be seen exquisitely-painted cups and saucers, tiles, and panels, wonderful needle-work on curtains, *portières*, table-covers, etc.—even tidies and d'oyleys that look like embroidered poems. But " frames decorated in color—except as mirror frames—and painted passepartouts, wax flowers and fruit, feather flowers, leather-work, skeletonized leaves, painted candles, knitting, crochet, Berlin-wool work, underclothing, or embroidered portions of it, and plain sewing, are excluded as inadmissible under the term of 'art;' also imitations of Limoges and other pottery, decorated with oil-color and varnish. An article which is not honestly what it purports to be cannot be considered a work of art."

Here, then, is an opening for the favored few whose work will pass the jealously-guarded portals; but, once within, appreciation and liberal remuneration are almost sure to follow. Exhibitors are not obliged to be pupils, nor to have an acquaintance with any member of the society to obtain the privilege of admission; but, unless introduced by a subscriber, a yearly entrance-fee of five dollars is demanded. Each one will receive, upon application, a number which will represent her work upon the books of the society, and which must be added to name and address in "business letters."

Nor is it necessary to live in the city in order to enter work at the Society of Decorative Art, the only stipulation in regard to distance being that "all work must be delivered to the society free of expense." Therefore, ladies living in the country, who are able to meet the requirements, have the same privileges in this respect as their city sisters.

China-painting produces, perhaps, the most popular and profitable results of any of the art studies; and almost any one, with an eye for color and some knowledge of drawing, can easily acquire it. A lady who had successfully practised ordinary drawing and painting, although quite self-taught, managed, in the course of a single day spent at the School of Design, to become sufficiently acquainted with the principles of painting on china to take up this delightful occupation on her return to her distant village home, to the satisfaction at least of herself and her friends.

The decoration of fans, now so much in vogue, is almost a branch by itself; but it is expressly stated by the Society of Decorative Art that articles of this nature, "to be received, must in all cases show special excellence in the combination of harmonious coloring and form, and the appropriateness of the decoration." Birds, butterflies, all *winged* creatures, are supposed to be particularly suited to objects that have such intimate relations with air—flowers have run riot over them for centuries—and figures have also been introduced with less good taste, perhaps, than any other device.

Some fans were beautifully ornamented lately with *pen-etchings*, resembling the finest engraving, by a lady whose tasteful fingers never seemed to make a mistake in this most delicate of undertakings. These dainty articles were in great request for Christmas presents among those who could afford to pay for them; and, in one instance, the fan, a very beautiful one of pale pink silk, with pearl handles, was furnished, and twenty dollars paid for the work alone. The artist confessed that she began her task with trembling fingers, fearful of spoiling the valuable article committed to her care; but courage came as the work progressed, and her labor was crowned with even more than its usual success.

Hand-screens, so indispensable since open fires and chimney-pieces have been made much of, also offer a wide field for decoration to those who can handle the artist's brush; and whether painted in rich colors, or delicately traced in sepia and India-ink, they are sure to be pretty and ornamental. Many of the Chinese and Japanese articles of this sort suggest ideas to be partly adopted and improved upon.

Plaques, either of china or smooth wood, are endless in design, and, when well-painted and handsomely mounted, make very satisfactory mural ornaments. Very beautiful designs for plaques are frequently the work of lady-artists, and prizes are sometimes offered for those of superior merit.

There are many remunerative pieces of work for those who can produce pleasing effects with color, although unable to attempt the higher walks of art—dinner-cards, neckties, and even buttons coming in for a share of ornamentation. A lady lately painted a set of the latter for a black silk dress with minute forget-me-nots; and the effect, enhanced by larger sprays of the same flower at each corner of the vest, was extremely pretty.

Some inventive genius originated the idea of medallion sets painted on silk of various colors over large button-moulds: necklace, ear-rings, brooch, bracelets, in one pattern of flowers; and, before they were too extensively imitated, they were thought very pretty and tasteful. They were quite profitable, too, to the artist, as they were quickly done; but they have had their day, and some other small invention, equally pretty, would receive as warm a welcome.

The painting of panels, for doors and rooms, has become an important industry, and brightness and beauty are fast taking the place of wooden monotony. Ladies who are gifted in executing pretty and unique designs of their own invention may almost be said to hold a fortune on the tips of their brushes.

One lady, at least, may be cited who, in this department of decorative art, has always as many engagements as she is willing to take, and at her own price.

Illustrations for books, if bright and original, are always in demand; and in writing for children, especially, pictures go a great way. It sometimes happens that two friends can use together pen and pencil—one writing, and the other illustrating; and, by combining these talents on the same piece of work, better results are accomplished than by working separately. A little sketch, or poem, sent to a periodical for children, if accompanied by an apt illustration, has *nine* chances of acceptance where an equally good article, without the picture, would have but *one*.

Occasionally, a delightful correspondent, whose letters are intended only for the eyes of personal friends, will illustrate the scenes or people she describes, with a few characteristic strokes, in such a life-like way that the scene or person is there before the reader; and these careless sketches, if published, would often put to shame the work of popular comic artists.

This inimitable gift, with the usual contrariety of fortune, is usually bestowed upon those who do not employ it, except for the amusement of themselves and their friends; but any one with a ready pencil for illustration has a direct way to money-making close at hand.

Chapter VIII.

HOUSE-DECORATION.

Two English Ladies.—The Decorator of the Past.—A New Field for Women of Taste and Judgment.—The Woman's Province.—How to Begin.—Conscientious Work.—A "House Beautiful."—Farther Suggestions.—A Pair of Vases.

The domain of art is wide, and offers a variety of employment to those who understand it, not only in creating, but in selecting and disposing of the creations of others.

The Misses Garrett, of London, have made a large and profitable business of *house-decoration* in painting, wood-work, and furniture — first fitting themselves for the undertaking by a thorough education in art, and exhibiting in their own house, with its admirably chosen belongings, sufficient proof of their qualifications. The arrangements of this house are described by visitors to be not only uncommonly beautiful, but beautifully uncommon. Of these belongings the owners can discourse delightfully for hours together; and they have published a small book on the subject of house-decoration.

Formerly, people who had money to spend on house-furnishing were satisfied to give a fashionable upholsterer *carte blanche* for the furnishing of the new house, with the laudable object of making it look as much as possible like other people's. But all that has been changed, and the furnishing of the present day aims at individuality. Art, of course, above and beyond everything, say the reformers; but, after this, let us be original. To have something that one's neighbors have not, and are not likely to have, is a positive happiness.

"Until lately," writes Miss Garrett, "a house-decorator (to all except the extremely wealthy) has meant simply a man who hangs paper and knows mechanically how to paint wood. In his proper place he would fulfil the part which a dispenser does to a doctor—he should be able faithfully to follow directions, and honestly to carry out instructions; and, as a rule, this *rôle* he is able to fulfil. But a decorator should mean some one who can do more than this; he should be able to design and arrange all the internal fittings of a house—the chimney-pieces, grates, and door-heads, as well as the wall-hangings, curtains, carpets, and furniture. All these it has hitherto been customary to intrust to different people, none of whom has had any part in the deliberations of the other. The consequence of such a disjointed arrangement has been that, in modern houses, one seldom finds a room which makes an harmonious whole."

These ladies are themselves able to meet all these requirements; but they are exceptional cases. There is no reason, however, why other ladies with an equal amount of taste, even though lacking their educational advantages, should not be able, in some measure, to fill the place of the Misses Garrett in this country. Wealthy people in our land of changes are constantly furnishing and refurnishing their houses; and many of them, having more money than taste, would gladly pay for the guidance of a cultivated eye and a ready perception of harmony and fitness.

House decorative art is one for which ladies are peculiarly fitted, but with which they have as yet had little to do.

"When a house, the very centre of a woman's kingdom, and the place where she spends most of her time, is to be furnished and decorated, men are called in to decide what hues shall prevail, what hangings and carpets, and other belongings, shall meet my lady's eyes day after day—often what pictures shall hang upon her walls, what books shall come, like silent friends, to take up their abode with her." This is not a man's business at all, but a woman's; and, if well-conducted *as* a business, it might be made very remunerative.

A lady employed as a house-decorator could present a plan or general outline of what she proposed to do—after carefully studying the capabilities of the rooms—with an estimate of cost, and submit it to the householder. The result would probably prove satisfactory to both parties; and one house tastefully furnished might be an excellent advertisement for future engagements.

The decorator should resemble the worthy Mrs. Gilpin in having "a frugal mind," wherever this virtue is desirable, and a nice calculation of expenditure; so that people of moderate means would find it more economical to have the benefit of her taste and judgment in furnishing than to take the responsibility themselves. Since the revival of the beautiful in ordinary things it is just as important to furnish the simple cottage harmoniously as the more pretentious mansion; and, as cottages are more numerous than palaces, the decorator would oftener be called upon to spend $500 than $5000—provided her charges were reasonable, and a gift for making one dollar do the work of two apparent to the dullest comprehension.

The two accomplished English ladies who have introduced such a reform in house-decoration preside over a charming establishment, where beautiful objects, collected with unfailing taste and judgment, may not only be admired but purchased; and any lady engaging in the same occupation would find a house capable of unique adornment a great advantage in this way. It could be quietly given out, among a circle of friends, that Mrs. ——'s rooms were charming—quite out of the common order—full of pretty effects produced at a moderate outlay; and one would bring another to look and admire—to buy a picture, perhaps, or the duplicate of a graceful hanging —and custom would thus flow in by degrees, until success was no longer doubtful.

A discreet amount of bric-à-brac could be taken on commission, and arranged with taste among the other furnishings; it would show to better advantage, and be more salable, than in the shop of the dealer. Lady-artists, too, amateurs "who paint only for amusement," would gladly contribute some of their best efforts to the adornment of Mrs. ——'s parlors, for she might, in time, be able to find purchasers for them.

The business is one that may be made quite extensive; for tradesmen and dealers of all kinds, desiring to bring their goods into notice, would probably furnish samples of them to be used and displayed by Mrs. ——. In this way the house could be furnished with little or no expense to the occupant. With responsible references as security, it would not be difficult to make such arrangements; and private parties, who wished to dispose of old and handsome articles, would greatly prefer an opportunity of this kind to the medium of the auctioneer or second-hand dealer.

A lady, engaged in quite a different occupation, once received a letter from a member of an old Southern family asking if she could dispose, on commission, of a pair of valuable china vases — an heir-loom from a great-great-grandmother. The vases were valued at two hundred and fifty dollars, and from the description must have been well worth it; but the person to whom the letter was written was obliged to decline the responsibility. The incident, however, made quite an impression, and the idea was evolved by degrees that, with the vases as a foundation, a very pleasant occupation could be organized, and one that would well repay all who were engaged in it.

Chapter IX.

SHOPPING ON COMMISSION.—AGENCIES.

Attractions of Shopping on Commission.—Profits Received.—Reasons for Decline.—Comparative Advantages of New York and other Places.—Necessary Qualifications.—Suggestions for a Circular.—Advertisements.—Shopping for Friends.—Book Agents.—A City Lady's Enterprise.—Characteristics of Agents.—Encouragement for Ladies.—Miss G——'s Experience.—The Catastrophe.—A Decided Contrast.—Munificent Emoluments.—Other Subscription-works.—An Agent by Proxy.—Small Wares.—Advantages of Knowing how to Work.

Shopping on commission is, for those who succeed in it, an extremely profitable employment; while there is a certain degree of pleasant excitement in receiving letters and selecting pretty articles. An indefinable charm seems to lurk in the spending of money, even if it is other people's; and the shopper by proxy enjoys this sensation to the fullest extent.

Sometimes city residents, as well as those who live in the country, are glad to have their shopping done for them, as it spares them much labor and perplexity; and those who are conscious of their own deficiencies in taste and judgment are especially glad to avail themselves of this relief. The commission charged to purchasers is five per cent.; and as merchants allow a discount of from six to ten per cent. to shoppers on commission, this makes a very handsome return to those who have a reasonable amount of orders.

A lady, who managed this department in connection with her other duties on a fashion periodical, received one hundred dollars a month from this source alone; but she complains that, within the last two or three years, the business has fallen off, so that only small and occasional orders are the rule now. She attributes this partly to the fact that all the dry-goods houses will now send samples to the remotest ends of the earth; while ready-made suits are so easy of attainment, that the resident of Kamtchatka, or the Philippine Islands, has only to "send waist and bust measure, length of skirt," etc., to be fashionably arrayed in as short a time as the machinery of the sewing-machine and ocean steamer can possibly accomplish it.

So many persons, too, have lately entered into the business of shopping on commission, that scarcely a periodical of any standing is to be found without one or two advertisements of this nature. New York is the most desirable centre for shopping, and the advertisements are almost invariably dated from thence; but, perhaps for this very reason, some other place, where articles of a peculiar or unique description are to be had, would be likely to attract customers. The experiment could, at least, be tried without involving much expense; but all preliminaries must be carefully arranged.

The first of these, perhaps, is to be sure of one's own powers—what amount of walking, or other fatigue, can be incurred without injury, and also the selection of a substitute in case of emergency. For orders of this kind frequently arrive at very *mal-à-propos* times, when the principal is either ill, or so engaged with other orders that it is impossible to attend to them at once. And the *at once* principle is of the greatest importance in this particular occupation.

The wording of an attractive circular, that shall yet be so thoroughly truthful that no exception can possibly be taken to a single item, after the arrival of executed commissions, is a point of no small weight. It is desirable to mention everything that one purposes to do, and yet to make the circular rather compressed than expansive; while a judicious choice of words and phrases will have much to do with securing customers of the best class. Half a dozen influential names as references are quite indispensable, as "orders are in all cases to be accompanied by the amount required."

An advertisement which has to be paid for word by word is not in danger of being too lengthy; the great difficulty is to say what seems necessary in so very confined a space. The charges for advertising are most unreasonable in many cases, and quite appal the impecunious beginner; but it is the experience of successful business men that advertising pays. A fictitious name, if accepted by those who are to be responsible for the advertiser's honesty and capability, may be substituted for the real one, and a post-office address given instead of the residence.

Some ladies have their leisure moments profitably employed by shopping for friends at a distance; and this can be done without the aid of circulars or advertisements. It lightens, too, the labors and perplexities of those unfortunates who, on a hurried visit to the city, are often obliged to waste much precious time and strength, and encroach upon limited trunk accommodation, to satisfy the demands made upon them often by mere acquaintances. The very fact of their going to the city seems a sufficient reason for their doing the shopping of the community; and weary feet, car fares, and loss of time are never taken into consideration. It would be well for those victims of imposition calmly to announce their intention of shopping on commission at every visit to the city, to defray their expenses thither; and, if this object were not accomplished, they would certainly find themselves in possession of their time.

In shopping for friends one has the advantage of knowing their individual tastes and needs; while the customers have the comfort of perfect confidence in the person to whom they intrust their money and purchases. When shopping is executed with taste and economy, it is almost worthy of being called an art; and a natural aptitude is indispensable to success in making it an occupation.

Among newspaper advertisements, those for agents of various kinds occupy much space and promise large pecuniary returns. Book-agents, in particular, for "the best selling work ever known," are greatly in demand; and if the statements could be credited, even with a discount, any one of "fair education and pleasing address," engaging in this occupation, might well feel on the high-road to fortune.

It is not a calling that commends itself to the shrinking and refined; and yet in some instances it has been taken up, as a temporary resort, by ladies belonging to this class with very fair success. "A hole may be the accident of a day, but a darn is premeditated poverty;" and, acting upon this principle, ladies who are in want of money for some special purpose often prefer a short, exciting, perhaps somewhat unpleasant, experience of this kind to a tedious apprenticeship at teaching, or a more permanent engagement in regular business. This has, at least, the advantage of being taken up and dropped at pleasure; it needs no previous preparation, and very little, if any, capital.

A story is told of "an educated New York lady who wished to earn a livelihood, and, not seeing any other way open, she became a book-agent. She got a horse and buggy, and rode through the country, and was very successful. She met with a young lady who was very anxious to join her. They made a great deal of money, and wrote a book of their travels."

It is a somewhat unusual thing to see an agent of any kind who looks like a lady or a gentleman, or who is interesting in any way; and for this reason, doubtless, they are connected in the public mind with tramps, and are often treated accordingly. Many of them deserve nothing better, as they are pertinacious and disagreeable to an incredible extent; and all the members of the same calling are obliged to suffer in consequence.

But a lady who undertakes this occupation in a lady-like manner will seldom fail to meet with respectful consideration, if not with subscribers; and, with the right book in the right place, she can also count upon the latter. An account of some actual experiences may serve to encourage the uninitiated who contemplate making a trial of their powers.

Miss G—— was a pretty, attractive girl, not at all accustomed to " roughing it;" but she found herself all at once most unpleasantly scant of money, and with an inconvenient fondness for the velvet and roses of life. Being of an enterprising turn of mind, and having no guardians to restrain her, she resolved to make a new departure of some kind; and, on the assurance of a respectable publisher that book-agents really *did* make money, she invested a dollar or two in a prospectus and started forthwith.

Calling herself by another name which began with the same letter, and bearing a letter of recommendation from the publisher to a minister in the country town which she had chosen for her first field of labor, the young lady went, on her arrival, to the hotel where she had been directed, and was fortunate enough to find already there the very minister she was in quest of. He was a courteous gentleman, and, taking Miss G——'s cause up vigorously, he recommended her book to the best people in the place, who, when she called upon them, were quite ready to become subscribers.

Having profitably exhausted A——, Miss G—— proceeded to the next town, with a letter of introduction from her clerical friend to a brother minister.

This gentleman and his wife kindly urged her to make their house her home during her sojourn in the place, and the young lady gladly accepted this hospitable invitation, which spared her from the exposure and dreariness of a hotel. A pleasant fortnight was spent at the parsonage, and eighty dollars cleared in money, besides a present to her kind entertainers; and, with two or three letters from these friends to people of note in the neighboring township, Miss G——resumed her travels.

The book she offered was the biography of a prominent and popular character, its tendency a good one, and hence it was always endorsed by clergymen; while its moderate price placed it within the reach of almost every one. The young agent found a pleasant reception everywhere, and received constant invitations to dinner and tea; was extensively questioned in regard to her motives for embarking in such an enterprise; while kind, motherly women gave her a great deal of good advice.

She never met with rudeness but once, and that was on a lonely country road; after that she carried a pocket-pistol for self-defence; and many a well-intentioned man, passing the girlish figure that tripped so gracefully along, little dreamed of the deadly weapon on which her hand rested, ready for immediate use. She never *did* use it, but it gave her a sense of protection to carry it.

After passing a winter and spring in her self-chosen occupation, Miss G—— found herself in possession of the comfortable little sum of nine hundred dollars. This was doing far better than she could have done in any other way, and she had enjoyed some very amusing experiences; but, notwithstanding her success, she decided to retire permanently from business. During her visit at the parsonage she met a professional gentleman, who manifested an especial interest in her; and, as this interest plainly increased during the winter—being expressed in the shape of letters and flying visits at the various points where the young lady stayed—it was finally returned, and ended, as such things usually do, in an engagement. "Culminated," however, would be a better word, as the interest has never ended at all, after several years of marriage.

Miss G——'s *trousseau* was bought with her earnings as book-agent; and she and her husband have had many a laugh over her adventures. But he always maintains that it was a dangerous step to travel under an assumed name, as some one who knew her might have appeared in the most unexpected place

—people have such a surprising faculty for turning up where they are least wanted—and this would have resulted most unpleasantly. The lady laughingly insists, however, that as no such person *did* appear, she took the wiser course in not having her real name associated with the *rôle* of a book-agent.

Miss Thorne was an altogether different person: severely plain, and with an aspect of always doing her duty, she was what some people call "well along" in the vale of single sisterhood. There was nothing frivolous in her attire or her speech, no suavity of manner, but a style of address that was most directly to the purpose. She looked like just what she was, a plain, sensible school-teacher; and it was evident that her success as a book-agent must depend entirely on the merits of the book—there was no personal magnetism about Miss Thorne with which to draw subscribers.

She was wonderfully successful, and that, too, with an old-fashioned religious work that she carried year after year, and that never seemed to lose its interest. But she went bravely under her own name—she was not in the least ashamed of it, because she was well-known and respected; and friends in one place passed her on to friends of theirs in another. She always knew just where she was going to stay beforehand; and each morning her list of calls was made out for the day.

Miss Thorne's accounts showed that she certainly cleared over $2000 a year; and her avowed object of making $10,000 before retiring seemed likely to be realized. She had an invalid sister, whom she boarded with some friends in the inland city where she had taught school; and to buy a comfortable home for this sister and herself was the end for which she worked.

Miss Thorne received the very maximum of percentage ever allowed to agents, the publishers of subscription books being eager to secure her services upon almost any terms—she was so eminently respectable; and people seemed to feel at once that her statements could be relied on. She never failed to deliver her books at the appointed time; and subscribers never failed to find them all that the prospectus represented them. Miss Thorne considered a substantial, well-known book the best investment for an agent; and she did not approve of carrying more than one work at a time. She received fifty per cent., or half the price of the volume; Miss G—— received forty. The latter is the ordinary commission; and occasionally it is a little less.

Subscription books are often published in numbers; but these are more troublesome to deliver, and involve more care and responsibility, than a single volume; people, too, are often suspicious of them, as they have been known to give out before the subject was finished. But, on the other hand, so small a sum of money is required at once that the total cost is scarcely felt; and this makes them quite popular. Servant-girls are particularly addicted to this kind of literature.

When some particular book or periodical is to be introduced into a parish or society, and a list of names is furnished belonging to people who are sure to want it, the position of agent, for some lady in want of money, is by no means unpleasant. Her subscribers are prepared for her visit, and, instead of regarding it as an intrusion, they are rather disposed to feel grateful to her for bringing them what they desire to have.

Agents are employed for many other things besides books; but a lady could scarcely undertake the sale of them in person, as it savors too much of the peddler. Many articles of general use meet with a ready sale in country villages— where, if they are kept at all, they are generally of inferior quality at a higher price.

A lady who wished to dispose of some small wares which, if sold, would yield her a good profit, went to a village hotel and engaged board for a week; then she requested the landlord to send her two or three bright boys who were anxious to earn some money. The boys appeared, glowing with expectation, and each one received a box of neck-ruffles, to be sold by the dozen at a very moderate price. With many exhortations to carry their burdens carefully, they were despatched in different directions; and, before many hours had elapsed, each boy had disposed of his stock and wanted another box. A small percentage on each dozen sold had roused their energies to excitement pitch; and the worthy villagers seemed in danger of being ruffled up to their eyes.

The work went briskly on for a week; by that time the neighborhood for two or three miles around was quite exhausted, and it was necessary to make a change of locality. The real agent had passed her time comfortably in her room, while her subordinates, like busy bees, improved each shining hour, and did all the work, both parties being thoroughly satisfied with the results of this arrangement. Ruches and ruffles are particularly salable wares in country places; they save so much trouble in the way of collars; and other small articles that would do equally well might be added at discretion.

Corsets, braces, etc., are frequently sold in this way; also fancy soaps and perfumery; and on articles of this kind a hundred per cent. is sometimes given to agents. It is undoubtedly a money-making business; and, when proper assistants could be found, an enterprising lady might make it very profitable, without doing more than advancing the capital and purchasing the goods.

The "directions" furnished to agents are often very comical, and of little use in the way of guidance. Those who study them most faithfully, and tax the memory with them for emergencies, do not acquit themselves half as successfully as do those who follow their natural promptings, and adapt their course to circumstances as they arise.

A horse and buggy, with a boy to drive, will be found almost indispensable, in the country, to the book-agent, and especially when a number of books are to be delivered; but these articles, boy included, can generally be hired by the day or half-day for a moderate sum, that does not count in comparison with the profits.

Chapter X.

GARDENING FOR PROFIT.

Advantages of a Country Residence.—Value of a Garden-patch.—What Has Been Done.—Want of Enterprise.—A Small Garden Well Managed.—What a Woman Might Do.—Opportunities in Fruit-raising.—The Capabilities of Currants.—A Condensed Strawberry Farm.—How to Start and Manage it.—Quinces to the Front.—Advantages and Drawbacks.—Fruit-growing Generally.

COUNTRY residents have, in many instances, greater advantages than their city friends in the way of opportunities for money-making; and among the most profitable rural and semi-rural occupations are the raising of flowers, vegetables, plants for medicinal and other purposes, the collecting and arranging of ferns and autumn leaves for ornamental uses, etc.; also the care of bees, poultry, and other live stock.

Many a careworn woman, struggling with her housework, and finding it next to impossible to make both ends meet, has only to look into her garden-patch and see there the foundation of a different order of things, which might easily be made to culminate in an able-bodied Bridget in the kitchen, a half-grown boy at work outside, and the lady herself engaged in the lighter occupation of sorting fruit and vegetables, or tying up plants. At another time she might be balancing her poultry accounts, or calculating her prospective honey—not forgetting the delightful employment of the "king in the parlor" who was counting out his money.

A popular writer relates the experience of two sisters, who found themselves sorely put to it for the means of living, in spite of owning a comfortable house and garden. A wise friend, who boarded with them, pointed out the garden as a source of revenue; and, somewhat incredulously, they adopted her suggestions.

A boy to keep the garden in order seemed to have come to them naturally with their other stock, and the boy was at once employed in gathering the vegetables daily and disposing of them in the village. It was already late in the summer when the experiment began, and the crops had been planted without reference to anything but home consumption, which prevented them from being so remunerative as they could easily have been made. The returns were, nevertheless, very encouraging, almost every day bringing a respectable income from corn, beans, tomatoes, etc.

It is a well-known fact that, in country villages, people who do not raise their own fruit and vegetables really suffer for want of them, being obliged to depend on the travelling huckster, or the nearest town, for what supplies they can get. And yet how seldom any one is found with sufficient enterprise to anticipate these needs, and raise fruit and vegetables purposely to supply them! Even so small a space as half an acre, if cultivated to its utmost capacity, and planted with popular vegetables for family use, would yield a fair return in money, besides supplying the owner with the most healthful of summer food.

An account of a small garden successfully managed may furnish encouragement to those who think they have too little land to cultivate for profit.

Originally a carrot-patch, part of it was then devoted to onions, and "all round the edge of the onion bed," says the owner, "planted with Wethersfield Red, I sowed parsley seed, and, between the rows of Carter's First Crop Pease we put in dwarf celery for a second crop after the last hoeing. Stout Anselm worked the ground with the horses, at the time of the carrot and other green crop hoeing, and made the headlands of potatoes. I procured strong-rooted currants and gooseberries, and planted them in rows wide enough apart for the horses to cultivate, and grew every kind of vegetable the first year, except asparagus.

"Since then, a bed of this has been made, and is the most eagerly sought and highly prized of them all. Two rows of strawberries, planted along the fence, supply us with mammoth Jocunda sufficient for preserves and a good table supply; while, by keeping our few raspberries cut back and trained to a trellis, we have the large fruit, and enjoy it better than any we could buy. The early Vermont potato is a superior variety, and we use early and late corn to prolong the season.

"It is astonishing how small a piece of ground will supply a family, if it is properly enriched, and attention paid to planting wide, with a view to a second crop. Radishes among beets are soon out of the way; so is lettuce among carrots; and at the same time this practice tends to keep the garden tidy and free from unsightly rubbish. I sowed some of the low-growing annual flowers along the sides of my vegetable beds, and their bright bloom was always before me when gathering anything for dinner.

"Turnips, I found, did well, even late, between the rows of onions, which were pulled up late in August and laid to dry. The turnip-fly does not seem to like the smell of onions, and left ours unmolested. And for the squashes, both summer and winter, which we grow, I found diluted cow-manure effectual in keeping off the bugs and strengthening the plants. Up the side of the house grows a Delaware grape-vine now; and half a dozen damson plum-trees, not far off, supply us with this choice preserve.

"I keep the rubbish in the compost-heap all winter, and make it the place for soap-suds and other good things; and when the pile is removed in spring to the garden, its removal leaves a rich spot, where one may safely drop a few melon and cucumber seeds; and, if covered with a pane of glass placed over a bottomless box, the melons ripen a week earlier than in the open air.

"Half a dozen tomato-plants put into a warm, dry, not too rich, corner supply us for first use; and a few later plants, a second crop for preserving and canning, may be put in after any of the early vegetables—spinach, beets, or radishes—are pulled. Cabbage and cauliflower are grown in small quantities, the trouble with the caterpillar being so great that we have to apply air-slacked lime several times; and then, if the plants chance to be neglected for a few days, we find the leaves are riddled.

"In spite of these drawbacks, however, the little garden was found to be a source of real profit, as well as pleasure; and almost any other well-cultivated plot could be made equally productive. The most timid of women in business enterprises, and with neither man nor boy in the family to depend on for help, might venture to hire sufficient labor to put her piece of ground in order, and plant it with fruit and vegetables—confident that she could dispose of enough, at least, to pay all expenses and keep her table well supplied. This of itself is *some-*

thing to accomplish; and there would be scarcely a doubt of her doing much more."

There are many small avenues of profit connected with fruit-raising that seem to be quite overlooked. The regular farmer or fruit-raiser considers them *too* small for his notice; and this is just where a woman, without much to invest, will find her opportunity.

For instance, almost every one wants currants, or what may be called the results of currants; they are useful in so many ways; and yet a few straggling bushes, that receive little or no attention, are the only evidences of their cultivation in ordinary places. Experience proves that they are comparatively little trouble to raise, and that a good harvest may be reaped from a small outlay. While abundantly paying the cultivator at three dollars a bushel, they are often sold for four dollars.

There is always a market for currants; and the fruit may be kept from the devastating worm by dusting the bushes with hellebore. To keep it also from the early bird, which catches a great many things besides the worm, it is safer to plant the white varieties—the bright gleam of the red fruit acting as a signal for a ready-made feast.

A successful cultivator advises planting for profit the White Dutch, Versaillaise, Cherry, and Victoria, and says: "The ground should be well-drained, in order to prevent frost-heaving, as the bush is easily pried out when there is much freezing and thawing, with little snow. My plan is to set the bushes in rows ten feet apart, and six feet in the row. Between the rows corn or any hoed crop may be planted. In the rows plant beans or potatoes. Cultivate and hoe the whole ground. Always slightly hill the currants at the second or last hoeing.

"It is a good plan to have a patch of gooseberries near the currants. The worms will appear first on the gooseberries, and can be promptly disposed of with two dustings of hellebore. They will then not appear to any extent, if at all, on the currants. It is best to apply the hellebore when there is dew on the bushes."

An acre or a half-acre of ground could be made in this way quite a source of profit, as a lady, besides disposing of the fresh fruit as opportunity offered, could convert the remainder into jelly and wine with still better results. The red currant is, in spite of the birds, a desirable variety to raise for manufacturing purposes, in view of the rich ruby color that makes the preserve attractive.

Several acres of currants would produce a handsome yield in every way; and a lady would find more remuneration and less care in devoting her energies to some particular item, for which there is a steady demand, than to attempt a little of everything.

Considering the acres of strawberries already cultivated for marketing purposes, and the expense and risk attendant upon a large enterprise of this sort, it might not be well for a lady to undertake it to any extent. There is a fascination about it, however, to women, ever since the time, some years ago, when two needle-women published their experience with an acre of strawberries, plainly showing that the hoe was mightier than the needle—the weeding and picking of a few weeks being rewarded tenfold more than the steady sewing of an entire year.

If cows could be made to give cream, one cream cow would pay better than five milk cows; and on this same principle a small strawberry-patch, under high cultivation, would yield a greater profit than an acre worked in the ordinary way. This strawberry-bed should be under glass (or a cheap substitute for it); and so little space would be really needed that it might even be located in a city yard. For the distinctive feature of these strawberries would be, not the quantity raised, but the quality, and also their being ready for use some time in advance of the ordinary market. If large and handsome-looking, and ripe by the first or middle of April, they could be disposed of at a high price to confectioners and private purchasers.

Where there is a strawberry-bed already planted, a portion can be selected as free from weeds as possible, and with all the plants young and healthy. A good coat of short, unfermented manure or droppings will greatly hasten the ripening of the fruit, besides increasing the yield; and the plants should then be protected with a sash. On very cold nights sash and bed should be covered with straw, old hay, or mats, to keep off the frost.

For the berries, Triomphe and Jocunda, planted in alternating hills in the same row, will be most satisfactory.

A bed may also be started by layering, from June till September, early and strong runners in small pots—when well-rooted to be transplanted to larger pots, and the soil so arranged as to make them grow most vigorously in the autumn. The soil for the bed should be very rich, but need not be more than six or eight inches deep; and the plants must be knocked very carefully out of the pots, not to disturb the roots, and set in the ground at the rate of about four to every square foot. The glass should then be put on, and great care taken to air properly in cold weather. The plants will also require an occasional watering, unless there are plenty of warm rains in February and March, during which the sash can be opened.

A very moderate piece of ground, scarcely more in size than a long, narrow flower-bed, treated in this way, and filled with the prepared plants about the middle of January, will produce a great many quarts of very fine berries by the first of April; and *fresh* strawberries at this season have been sold as high as five dollars a quart.

The strawberry experiment, on this

high culture plan, is certainly worth trying.

The quince is a neglected fruit that seems to offer large possibilities to the patient cultivator; and the convenient size of its low, spreading trees—mere bushes, in fact—renders it an easy subject for a lady to undertake. Independently of its fruit, it is a pretty shrub, not half appreciated, with velvety-petaled blossoms of the palest pink, as becomes a member of the rose family, to which it belongs; and, even if not useful, it might justly be regarded as ornamental.

But who has not a weakness for quince preserves, when properly made? For marmalade, jelly, and crystallized quarters of the fruit, and *baked quinces?* These condiments, or confections, are always appreciated to the fullest extent; yet the market supply of quinces is small, and almost any other fruit-bearing tree seems more popular with the growers of fruit.

If the quince were a tree of wayward and perverse inclinations, repaying with base ingratitude the cultivation bestowed on it, and showing "nothing but leaves" in time of fruit, this state of things would be easily explained; but no fruit improves more under culture, or makes a better return for the time and care bestowed upon it. "While the visitor at agricultural and horticultural fairs," says some one, "may see large and varied collections of the best apples, pears, peaches, grapes, and other fruits, the collections of quinces are, in the majority of instances, confined to a few plates stored away on the back shelf, or in some out-of-the-way corner, where they are seen by but few others than the judges, and sometimes hardly by them. This indicates that fruit-growers and owners of orchards generally give but little attention to its cultivation; and that people at large do not appreciate it to the degree it deserves."

Perhaps people at large would appreciate it if it were properly cultivated and presented to their notice; and this is one of the departments of horticulture which an enterprising woman might engage in with the most encouraging results. She could have a quince orchard, whether large or small; and she might find it more profitable to send out her fruit in the shape of preserves than to supply the raw material. Even the few, straggling, neglected trees in the ordinary garden will repay scraping and cleansing and thorough cultivation.

The insect pests, from which the quince suffers, can generally be disposed of by applying a strong solution of soap-suds to the trunk and larger branches early in the spring, and several times during the summer. The borer, if still aggressive, may be exterminated by watching for the appearance of sawdust on the ground near the trunk of the tree, and when found, punching wire into its hole, or carefully cutting it out. If the trees are thoroughly examined in September the borer's life may be cut short in its youth.

The business of fruit-growing is one that has been successfully managed by ladies, who have found health and strength as well as profit in their calling; but there is still abundant room for fresh enterprise, if directed to some special quarter which has not yet been the object of general attention. And this is an important element of success in almost any business undertaking.

Chapter XI.

AMONG THE FLOWERS.

Scarcity of Women Florists.—First Steps.—Building a Greenhouse.—Economical Plans.—Variety not Desirable.—A Rose Garden under Glass.—Exterminating Insects.—Heliotrope.—A Market for Cut Flowers.—Ferns, Autumn Leaves, Grasses, etc.—A Corner Ornament.

THAT there should be so few women florists is often a subject of comment, as the care of flowers seems a calling peculiarly adapted to those who are supposed to have a natural love for the beautiful. Women will often cherish a few plants under endless household difficulties, but how seldom a man ever troubles himself about anything so unpractical! Yet the florists are almost invariably men, engaged in a business which women could conduct as well, or better.

Perhaps the question will come, Why don't they try it, then? and an answer may be found in the fact that the class of men who become florists is an entirely different one from the class of women who would be attracted to the occupation. The men usually begin as working gardeners, attaining by degrees the height of their ambition—to "set up" for themselves—and from long intimacy with work, not being in the least afraid of it, they are armed for all emergencies. They have also accumulated capital by degrees; while the lady begins as a lady, hemmed in by conventionalities and crippled by want of capital.

"Yes," responds Ysolte, "that is exactly *my* case; how do you advise *me* to set about becoming a florist?"

For a first step, perhaps, the most sensible proceeding would be to visit some successful gardener and ask his advice. If benevolently disposed (and people usually are in such cases), he will give all necessary information, and state his opinion on the chances of success in any particular locality. A very good idea of the expenses and disappointments attendant upon the raising of flowers, and the profits to be expected from their sale, may be obtained from him; but he will say at once that a florist, to continue the business throughout the year, must build a greenhouse.

He will also say that this, with proper heating apparatus, costs from $1000 to $1500, which will decide you at once to give up all idea of undertaking it.

Do nothing of the kind; but measure off your ground, engage your carpenter, and go in quest of a sash and blind factory. Here you may purchase second-hand sashes for half or one-third the cost of new ones; and you will find these articles the most expensive part of your greenhouse.

There is a great difference in greenhouses, both in appearance and cost. If of the "lean-to" order—which means having but one sloping glass roof, facing the south, and with covered sheds on the north side—the cost will be comparatively small; but, as a rule, the more sunshine the more flowers.

"Well, ma'am," said a worthy gardener, "they don't cost much, if ye builds 'em cheap. I gets a carpenter to build mine, and has 'em made kinder rough and cheap. They don't last as long, not more'n six years, but they *does* grow the flowers. I generally calculates to pay for 'em in two years, and when they tumbles down I builds another."

This would be the best kind for a lady's venture, and if she could have the work done at a season when carpenters, instead of being driven, are usually glad of a job, it would cost still less. A long, low building is better than a high one, as it is more convenient for handling the plants, besides insuring more sunshine. The size of the greenhouse would, of course, depend on the amount and variety of stock to be accommodated in it; and, in this particular, the advice of a practical florist is highly desirable.

The great fault of amateur greenhouse experiments is an ambition to raise all kinds of flowers in one small space; and, when the greenhouse is built for profit, this is a certain cause of failure. To select one kind of flower alone, and concentrate all the arrangements on developing it to the highest degree of perfection of which it is capable, would yield better returns and save much care and distraction of thought.

There can never be too many roses.

They are called for at all seasons of the year, and will bring a good profit to the grower at the lowest market prices; when selling at their *best* they are the most desirable of commodities. There is something particularly attractive in the idea of a *rose house*, which seems quite beyond an ordinary greenhouse; and a lady could manage such an undertaking not only with profit but with pleasure.

The best way of carrying out such a plan would be to have a rose garden arranged for summer, and covered with glass at the approach of cold weather. Having the roses planted in beds instead of pots reduces the labor of cultivation, saves the expense of pots, and seems to agree better with the plants. Two of the loveliest and most profitable roses for this purpose are the *Sofrano* and *Bon Silene;* the *Sofrano* being in demand both for funeral and wedding orders, while the *Bon Silene* is equally popular for its brilliant color and delicate fragrance. Both yield an abundance of bloom.

Care and thorough fumigation with leaf tobacco, of the poorest and cheapest kind, will effectually disperse the greedy insects that make rose life miserable and exhaust the patience of the much-tried florist. Sprinkling with fine Scotch snuff will often kill small insects, and this remedy is less troublesome than smoking. With perseverance in routing these active enemies, a rich soil, neither wet nor dry, and abundant sunshine, success in rose cultivation seems assured.

The heliotrope requires the same conditions and treatment as the rose; and, as it is a constant bloomer and much in demand for its delicious fragrance, a number of plants could be cared for in the rose house with very little more trouble. Roses and heliotropes together would provide a constant succession of bloom, and a very comfortable income for the cultivator.

The object of the little greenhouse here described is to raise flowers for city emporiums, which can, within an ordinary distance, easily be sent in boxes, and look as fresh, with skilful packing, as though gathered from plants close at hand. The lady among her roses at home has nothing farther to do with their sale, except to receive a handsome remuneration for labor that is in itself a pleasure.

In connection with the little greenhouse may be carried on another pleasant and profitable occupation—that of collecting and preparing ferns, autumn-leaves, vines, mosses, etc., for winter decoration.

The most successful locality for either of these employments would be in or near a large town rather than a city, as the former would afford a better market with less competition. All the bright-colored leaves, the various native ferns, some wild vines, mosses, and even flowers, if prepared so skilfully as to retain their beauty at least through *one* season, are quite in demand; and while many enjoy gathering and preserving them for themselves, others do not have the same opportunity, or are disinclined to take the trouble.

Great care and deftness and taste are all required to bring this work to perfection; and only by doing it in the most thorough manner, that will preserve the brightness and beauty of these natural ornaments, without making them look in the least artificial, can any degree of remunerative success be attained.

Originality and durability of treatment will meet with a just reward; and to avoid all appearance of *stiffness* in things from which all life has been pressed out is the triumph of skill.

A tall, gracefully-shaped vase—which, for this purpose, could be painted a dull Indian-red, or have cambric of this color drawn tightly over it—filled with plumes of feather-grass, cat-tails, thistle-pompons, milk-weed-pods, and seed-vessels of various kinds, artistically mingled with ferns, bright leaves, and vines, would be a very simple corner ornament, and yet a very salable one. The vase should be large enough to stand on the floor, while its contents should reach half way to the ceiling.

This is only one of many suggestions that might be made; for the capabilities of leaves, ferns, etc., are infinite.

Chapter XII.

BEES AND POULTRY.

Recommendations of Bee-culture.—Profit in Keeping Bees.—A Lady's Testimony.—Two Western Girls.—How to Prevent Stinging.—"How am I to Begin?"—Swarming Prevented.—Wintering Bees.—Making Honey from Sugar.—Pink Honey.—Profits from Hens.—Accommodation for Poultry.—General Care.—A Frenchwoman's Experience.—Roses and Honeysuckles.—French Soil.—Horse-flesh as Food.—Artificial Hatching.—The Barn-yard Fowl.—A Paying Business.—Rules for Successful Poultry-raising.—Spring Chickens.—Pigeons.—Proper Shelter.—Dutchies, or Common Runts, most Profitable.—A Flock of Turkeys.—Causes of Failure.—Delicacy of Young Turkeys.—Carefulness in Feeding.—Ducks and Geese.

THE culture of bees seems to accord naturally with the culture of flowers; and, in connection with a garden, it is a comparatively easy matter to raise bees.

They take up little room, generally "find" and take care of themselves, and have not, like poultry, a morbid appetite for seeds and summer vegetables. Bee-raising particularly commends itself to ladies, because there is so little labor involved in it; it is like having a colony of small slaves at work, while the owner is occupied with other things, or enjoying the sweet do-nothingness that comes of accomplished tasks or abundant means.

That bees are a great source of profit abundant experience proves; and, as they do not require private acres for promenading, they may be kept to advantage even in the city. But they are never found there; and, even in the country, it is very rare to find a *lady* engaged in keeping them to any extent. And yet they are the best paying investment in live stock that can possibly be made *as an incidental occupation*, which is just the subject in question—affording large returns for a moderate outlay, and involving very little after-expense.

It is stated in an agricultural report that a lady bought four hives for $10, and in five years she was offered $1500 for her stock, and refused it as not enough. In addition to this increase in her capital, in one of these five years she sold twenty-two hives and four hundred and thirty pounds of honey. On the strength of this, the writer declares that almost any woman in the city, as well as in the country, can manage bees, and make more profit than in any other employment requiring so little time and labor.

Two girls in Michigan are said to be successfully engaged in bee-keeping; they have fifty swarms of bees, and have sent recently to market eleven thousand pounds of honey, worth $3000. Here, adds the narrator, is a new employment for many girls, who could make a good living in this business.

The most serious objections to bees are stinging and swarming; but, in regard to the former, Italian bees, which are the most profitable and desirable in every way, are said also to be amiable, and not at all disposed to sting. Besides, a French scientific journal has published "a safe and convenient method" of getting the honey from the hives. A quarter of an ounce of chloroform is poured upon a handkerchief, which is laid on a plate resting upon a sheet or table-cover spread on the ground. An iron gauze sieve is then laid upon the sheet over the plate. The hive is carefully lifted from the bench and set upon the sieve; the sheet is drawn closely around the hive, to enclose the fumes of the chloroform. A loud buzzing ensues, to which succeeds perfect silence. Then the hive may be lifted, when the bees are found insensible, lying upon the sieve. The robbery is then proceeded with, the hive replaced, and in a short time the bees, revived by the air and sunshine, return to their hive and their labor as if nothing had happened.

"But how am I to begin?" asks the bewildered reader; "what is done *first?* I never was near a hive of bees in my life!"

The best beginning is to read some excellent work on the subject, like Quimby's "Mysteries of Bee-keeping;" then to follow some very practical instructions. "Get from one to four hives, according to your honey field and faith; take them to a bee-keeper, who will place a good first swarm in each hive, and remove them home. Or, if the seller is pleased to let them stand till fall, place boxes on them and let them stand till then. At the proper time in the fall remove the boxes, and take all home. With hives so constructed as to prevent the disposition to swarm, and the number limited to the capacity of the field, they would sometimes yield honey to the amount of two hundred pounds a hive in one season. On this plan there is little to do but to place and remove the boxes at the proper time. If the hive is so constructed as to give ample room in the breeding and wintering apartment, feeding is rendered unnecessary.

If proper means are used to give room in the surplus boxes for all the colony the whole season, before any preparation is made for swarming, and the hives are effectually shaded from the sun, no watching for swarms will be required, and no time necessarily devoted to them but to put on the surplus boxes in season and remove them when full; and this may be done by a neighbor accustomed to the business, if one is apprehensive of danger in performing these or any other operations about the hive."

This removes the second objection to bee-keeping, and reduces it to a very simple affair. These busy insects, however, are quite fastidious about their surroundings, and do not like the direct rays of the sun. An orchard seems to furnish the right degree of shade, and a bee-keeper says that the best success he has ever known with bees has been in orchards and shaded door-yards. In point of situation, elevated ground is better than a low place or valley.

Wintering bees is a far more serious matter than summering them, as swarms not properly cared for come out in the spring in a weak and dying condition.

The difficulty often arises *where* to winter them: out-of-doors, or in — above-ground, or down in the cellar. They require an even temperature of about forty degrees, and this is thought by the most successful bee-keepers to be best attained by cellar-wintering. "Others prefer out-door wintering, in which the bees are kept either in a so-called chaff hive, which has double walls, from four to eight inches apart, with the intervening space filled with chaff; or else the ordinary hives are surrounded by boards or a box, and the space between, which should be a foot wide, is filled with chaff or straw. In both cases the arrangements are such that the bees can fly whenever the weather is warm enough to induce flight."

Making honey from sugar has been successfully tried: fifteen pounds of white sugar being made into a sirup and fed to one of the experimenter's best stocks. The sugar was dissolved in little more than a pound of warm water. From a hole in the back part of the hive the bees entered into a tight box, and into this box the sirup was poured, covered with a thin board perforated with small holes, through which the bees could take up the sirup, and the board would settle down as the supply was exhausted. Over the box was placed a pane of glass, in order to watch the operations of the bees, and know when they required more sirup.

At the beginning of the experiment the box on the top of the hive had one small comb, but it was empty. The sugar was dissolved as the bees needed it, and they took it up so fast that, at the end of twenty days, the fifteen pounds had disappeared. There were twenty pounds of honey though in place of it, and this was sold for thirty cents a pound. The sugar cost $1 80, and the honey brought $6 00—the profit all being the result of bee-labor in the short space of three weeks.

The speculator adds: "The honey was most excellent, and I believe no one could have told the difference between it and the wild-flower honey. I shall try it again next fall, and I will flavor the sirup with a little tea, which I shall make from white clover-heads, and also add a little brandy, of which the bees are very fond."

A lady could make her honey very attractive by putting it up in some novel and tasteful way, and a beautiful pink tint may be imparted to it by giving the bees a little cochineal. As an ornamental dish for the table, in a handsome glass receptacle, it is unsurpassed; and a wreath of clover blossoms and leaves around the edge would be both pretty and suggestive.

A lady in Massachusetts has found it profitable to keep hens. Beginning with about sixty fowls in the spring, she raised from these four hundred and fifty chickens. During the season she sold $90 worth of eggs, and from the last of September to the last of January she sent to market a hundred and fifty pairs of chickens, which brought $260—making $350 in all.

A Pennsylvania farmer sold from *thirty* hens, in one year, eggs and chickens amounting to $430 78. The cost of feed and commissions for selling came to $161 84—leaving a net profit of $268 94. Another farmer acknowledged that "he had sold eggs as low as ten cents a dozen, and made money on 'em at that."

"Few people," writes a poultry-keeper, "think it worth while to spend money in furnishing suitable accommodations for their hens, or time in looking after them. In too many cases among farmers the fowls are obliged to find their own accommodations, and have to put up with what happens to offer, whether comfortable or not. Where fowls have to resort to trees, fences, carts, pig-pens, wood-pile, or what not, for roosts, they have not suitable accommodations; when they have to make their nests in hay-mows, under stacks, in the weeds, or other out-of-the-way places, they are not treated as they should be. When the feeding is irregular and spasmodic, sometimes too much, at other times too little; when the water supply is furnished for the most part only when it rains, or by stagnant pools or ditches, the owner is inviting cholera and other diseases. Poultry kept in this way will not be profitable; and the same may be said of any other kind of stock. There is more clear profit, however, to be derived from a well-bred flock of poultry, when systematically looked after, than from any investment of an equal extent in the whole line of legitimate husbandry."

A story is told of the experience of a French woman who was left a widow in very straitened circumstances, with four children to educate and provide for. All her attempts so far to improve her fortunes had failed, to her utter discouragement. Happening to stop one day at a small town where an agricultural fair was in progress, she followed the crowd, and became very much interested in what she saw. Wandering to the poultry enclosure, she was soon preoccupied with chaotic visions, until, finally, a country gentleman approached her, and began to discourse upon fowls.

Poultry exhibitions, he said, never satisfied him, and with fancy breeds he had no patience; the *common hen*, properly cultivated, was worth them all put together. While listening politely to the quaint speaker, the baroness perfected in her mind a plan which involved the education of hens, and promised a solution of her difficulties.

The result was a poultry enterprise of such magnitude as to be quite beyond the reach of ordinary aspirants; but it yielded a handsome income to the far-seeing French woman. The gradual steps, however, by which she reached such a pinnacle of success are not made visible, which is a serious loss to the reader in quest of information; and the baroness in this narrative passes at once from an impecunious condition to the ownership of an expensive establishment. No one knows whether she began with ten fowls or fifty, nor where she got the money to begin at all; there is only the broadly-stated fact that she successfully managed over thirteen hundred, and provided them with palatial quarters.

The building that accommodated these fortunate feathered charges is represented as having first and second stories divided into compartments. On the ground-floor were hatching-room, kitchen, grain-room, and store-room for eggs—the necessity for a kitchen having arisen from the custom of cooking much of the food. The second story had a wide veranda, or gallery, attached, with a railway and turn-tables at the corners. This was a great aid to the work; and every morning the four upper compartments were thoroughly cleaned—the nests and boxes once a week.

This wonderful poultry-house even had venetian shutters back and front, to insure perfect ventilation—which, with cleanliness, is the best protection against vermin. In the coldest weather the shutters were not quite closed, as the building was comfortably warmed by hot-air pipes from the furnace-range in the kitchen.

Care was also taken to give the fowls ample space for exercise; and this was secured by parks or yards of an acre and a half, extending from the four compartments. These were planted with a constant supply of green food, to keep the poultry in good condition; and the yards were separated by thick hedges, which extended to the pillars of the veranda. Nothing that would add to the comfort and well-being of the feathered inmates seemed to have been forgotten; and a large shed in each yard was always supplied with dry sand, that the fowls might "powder themselves" even on rainy days.

Masses of shrubbery were planted here and there in the yards, to protect the fowls alike from the rain and from the heat of the summer sun; and the fruit of the gooseberry and currant bushes adds a pleasant variety to their diet. Some elder-bushes originally planted in these parks were obligingly pulled up and replaced by raspberries, because it was found that the odor of their flowers was not agreeable to the hens! They condescended to eat the raspberries as fast as they ripened.

This sounds unmistakably French; but it had much to do with the good condition of the baroness's poultry that their dwelling-place was entirely free from the close, disagreeable odor peculiar to hen-houses. There came instead, through the venetian blinds, the perfume of roses and honeysuckles, with which the veranda-pillars were covered. "Why not flowers?" asked the gentle trainer of hens; "they cost nothing, and all creatures must, in some degree, be susceptible to æsthetic surroundings."

A special park was provided for the little chickens, where they were supplied with everything that well-conducted young fowls are supposed to want: fresh grass, plenty of fat insects, shade, and quiet. The eggs were not hatched artificially, nor were any fancy breeds to be found among these nursery inmates, the education of the common barn-yard fowl having proved entirely successful.

The principal object of this immense establishment was the exportation of eggs; and these were produced in such quantities as to yield a handsome income above all expenses.

There is said to be something in the nature of French soil—the presence of silex in considerable quantities—which makes the hens such wonderful egg-producers; but a writer who has studied the subject thinks that the absence of this quality might be made up by artificial means.

A man, living also in the vicinity of Paris, was represented as making $175,000 a year from the sale of eggs and fowls. His poultry was not treated like that of the baroness, being fed, for economy's sake, on horse-flesh, and lodged more practically and less picturesquely. All the old hacks of the city were purchased and slaughtered for food; and, by selling the skin, hoofs, etc., enough was realized to pay for the whole. The flesh was cut from the bones and converted by a machine into mince-meat; it was then slightly seasoned and put up in casks, which were sent by railroad to the egg-farm—about twenty-two horses a day being used for this purpose. The fowls delighted in this food, and would lay an egg a day in all seasons.

The sheds, offices, and other portions of this establishment were built around a quadrangle enclosing about twenty acres, which formed the general feeding-ground. This was divided by fences of open paling, only a limited number of fowls being allowed to herd together, and arranged in compartments according to age. Four years was the limit of existence.

Before marketing, the fowls were put into the fattening coops for three weeks, and sent alive to Paris. A hen was never allowed to sit. The breeding-rooms were warmed by steam to the same heat as that evolved by the hen while sitting. "A series of shelves, one above the other, formed the nests, while blankets were spread over the eggs to exclude any accidental light. The hatched chicks were removed to the nursery each morning, and fresh eggs laid in to supply the place of empty shells. A constant succession of chickens is thus insured; and, besides, the feathers are always free from vermin."

These, too, were the old-fashioned barnyard fowl. Their flesh is far more delicate than that of the prize varieties. The inference seems plain that the more animal food given, the more eggs, as the production of eggs always falls off at the season when insects disappear. Half an ounce a day of fresh meat, chopped as for sausages, is a sufficient allowance for one hen.

No one was ever known to keep fowls *understandingly* and say that it did not pay; and some enterprising American lady might do equally as well as the French baroness. She could begin with a flock of from fifty to one hundred; and, as the profit on each thoroughly cultivated hen often reaches the sum of $3 00 a year, an investment in poultry can scarcely fail to be a paying one.

Fowls are not so easily kept as bees, as they require room to range in, and never thrive so well in confined quarters. A person of experience says: "I am inclined to think that one thousand may be profitably kept under one roof, and with a few acres of forage-run, by adhering to the following rules:

"1st. Let the roosting-house be of ample size, giving each fowl about two feet of perch room, and having it so ventilated in winter that the air shall be pure. A ventilator in the roof is not sufficient; there must be windows to open (slide down from the top), according to the state of the weather.

"2d. Ample shed-room, connecting with the roosting-house, to give the fowls a chance to be protected from storms, and where a supply of water, gravel, old mortar, pounded charcoal, ground oyster-shells, etc., is within easy reach.

"3d. The business to be fully understood, and the fowls kept free of lice; feed to be corn, oats, buckwheat, and wheat-screenings, with boiled potatoes and meal occasionally, mixed with cayenne pepper, to be given hot in winter. Of course, I cannot give a hundredth part of all I *might* say on the subject in this article, but I will give general principles.

"In regard to raising early chickens and later fowls for market, I have space to say but little; but 'there is money' in that branch of the business, and a good deal, too, if it be rightly managed. Early chickens, weighing about a pound each, will command $1 50 a pair in New York in July; and the market has never been glutted with such young poultry."

Pigeons are usually associated with half-grown boys, who are given to spasmodic experiments with them of a commercial character, which never appear to result in much ready coin. But to those who understand them there is considerable profit in pigeons.

They are not at all difficult to understand, nor are their wants in any way complicated. A corner of a barn-loft will answer for lodgings; and in summer they will find their own provisions. Almost the only care they need is to clean the loft out twice a year. A frequent cause of failure with pigeons is to be found in the fact that, instead of fitting up a small loft with nests *inside*, boxes are nailed to the outside of the barn, and the squabs perish from being exposed to the inclemency of the weather.

In winter pigeons will feed with the poultry. They will raise on an average eight or nine pairs of young in a year, which will find ready sale when four weeks old at fifty cents a pair. In winter they will bring seventy-five cents. If the stock consists of Dutchies, or common runts, at a cost of $2 50 a pair, squabs twice the size of common ones can be raised, and these will, of course, command a proportionately higher price. Birds of the common variety, which cost only fifty cents a pair, will pay for themselves within two months.

Turkeys, too, are profitable on the

same conditions that are necessary in regard to hens—care and intelligence.

A flock of well-grown turkeys, according to a rural paper, make such an agreeable addition to the receipts of the farm, and they are often raised with so little trouble, that the seeming indifference of so many farmers with reference to them is something to be wondered at. The rules for breeding are simple and easily understood; and failures are due to two prominent causes: one, the weather, which in some seasons puts at fault the utmost possible care; the other, negligence.

"A hot and dry season is almost an essential for success with turkeys. This is so important that it is of little use to be in haste to get turkeys hatched early, as with chickens; though old birds are tough enough, young ones are exceedingly tender. If brought out by the first of June, it will generally be early enough. Even if they live through such chilly and damp weather as is common in May, they will not grow much until hot weather and bugs come to their relief; but let them hatch out in June, in weather which drives the breeder to the shade, and little turkeys just enjoy it; they will stretch themselves in the sun, and 'lay off' with every token of delight. Damp, chilly weather is their ruin; rain, abomination; morning dew, a poison sure to blight the hopes of inexperienced or careless breeders. Turkeys must be allowed to range very freely to insure success, but not while the grass is wet; that is, during the first two months or so of their lives. After that, one need not be quite so particular."

These little turkeys require an unlimited supply of varied, fresh, green food, especially lettuce, dandelion leaves, dock, young nettles, and onion tops; and they must be fed entirely on soft food for some weeks, gradually introducing grain in small portions for the first few months.

With care, a large number of turkeys may be profitably kept on a farm; and, during the winter season, there is always a demand for them in the market.

Ducks and geese are also desirable as sources of profit, where there is abundant room; and on a large, well-watered farm they will thrive to the best advantage.

Chapter XIII.

A FEW LAST WORDS.

The Value of Small Things.—Suggestions in Newspaper Paragraphs.—A Novel Pattern for an Auger.—Oyster and Snail Shells.—Improved Milk and Butter.—Profit in Tea-packing.—A Little Tea Store.—Cultivation of Mushrooms.—A Lady's Invention.—A Need to be Supplied.—Knowing What to Do.—Wasted Energy.

AMONG the numerous suggestions for money-making contained in these pages, many out-of-the-way industries and inventions have been left unnoticed. A very little thing will sometimes lead to wealth, while large enterprises fail; and observation and ingenuity are often of more value than the most plodding industry.

Paragraphs in the daily papers are

very suggestive, and two or three clipped at random will show what may be done in out-of-the-way fields.

Ransom Cook, of Saratoga Springs, who recently died at the age of eighty-seven, got his plan for making an auger that would bore at an angle with the grain (without starting with a gouge) by examining the lips of the worm commonly known as the "wood borer" with a microscope; and from this he made his model, which proved a perfect success.——Among the minor industries of Paris is the utilization of oyster and snail shells. Keepers of eating-saloons are required by law to put these shells in boxes by themselves, ready to be carried away by a person who has made a contract with the city for them. The oyster-shell is used often instead of mother-of-pearl in the manufacture of various fancy goods.

The *Toledo Blade* says there is a speedy fortune in store for some man who will open a shop in Toledo devoted to the specialty of pure milk and high-grade butter—kept conscientiously up to the standard, and offered to the public at from twenty-five to fifty per cent. above the market rates.——A good business may be done by purchasing certain articles in their original packages, and putting them up in a more desirable form. A firm in Philadelphia has made a fortune by repacking teas for miners' use, and shipping them to California and Australia.——The tea business is very profitable; and a tasteful little store, with a few cheap Chinese oddities in addition to the tea, could be managed by proxy, like the lunch-room, and made to yield a very respectable income.——Raising mushrooms is a regular occupation in France, and a Frenchman is now said to be in treaty for the use of the Mammoth Cave, Kentucky, for this purpose. It is an industry that may be carried on in almost any cellar, and will find a market in every large city.——A lady who invented some attachment to a sewing-machine made her fortune by it; and there is room for other attachments and improvements, and other fortunes.——If some ingenious woman will invent a button that will stay on boots, or something more comfortable and lasting than the fasteners now in use, she will reap a large pecuniary harvest.

One of the great arts of money-making consists in the gift of knowing just what to do, according to one's powers and circumstances; and we cannot better take leave of our subject than by quoting some excellent thoughts on wasted energy from the columns of a newspaper:

"Nobody can critically observe the structure of American social or domestic life without being struck by the immense amount of energy which is wasted in the woman's half of it.

"In any case the American man finds ample outlet for his energies. With the average woman it is different. She, too, recognizes the value of money: if poor, she wants to make it, and her anxiety to do this battles perpetually with her desire to do nothing which is strong-minded and unlady-like. How many hundreds of thousands of women in inland towns and country places, this August, are painting china, embroidering towels with hideous sunflowers, sketching that most ubiquitous of bores, the limp, mediæval woman in her poke bonnet, or sending off voluminous manuscripts, all in the hope of earning money secretly! She does not earn it. Her energy is wasted because she does not know how to bring it to bear. She is an amateur dabbler in half a dozen different arts, instead of a painstaking, conscientious worker in one little, unpretentious craft. Conscientious work in one direction will always bring wages in the end. In provincial communities, too, custom and prejudice are strongly opposed to the earning of money by women who rank as "ladies," except as artists and authors. Her energy is new wine in old bottles. The bottles do not break, but the wine is apt to turn sour and musty.

"The mistake made by all these women whose energy is running to waste is, that their aims are too wide and too vague. A living is to be earned, not by general amateur, ladylike "pottering," as Carlyle grimly calls it, but by a definite trade or craft, followed accurately and openly. The power of an unmarried woman is in danger of growing diseased from want of outside objects; the more reason, therefore, she should turn it away from herself. The poor she has always with her; and by the poor is not meant only the penniless, but the crippled, blind, and dumb of soul. A sufficient aim for such a one, too, is to fill the place and fulfil the duties of a gentlewoman in a mixed community, such as that of our American towns. But few of our American women realize that simple duty, and we see the results in the communities."

THE END.

INTERESTING BOOKS FOR WOMEN.

BEAUTY IN DRESS. By Miss Oakey. 16mo, Cloth, $1 00.

BEAUTY IN THE HOUSEHOLD. By the Author of "Beauty in Dress." Illustrated. 16mo, Cloth. (*In Press.*)

THE BAZAR BOOK OF THE HOUSEHOLD. Marriage, Establishment, Servants, Housekeeping, Children, Home Life, Company. 16mo, Cloth, $1 00.

THE BAZAR BOOK OF DECORUM. The Care of the Person, Manners, Etiquette, and Ceremonials. 16mo, Cloth, $1 00.

THE BAZAR BOOK OF HEALTH. The Dwelling, the Nursery, the Bedroom, the Dining-Room, the Parlor, the Library, the Kitchen, the Sick-Room. 16mo, Cloth, $1 00.

BAZAR COOKING RECEIPTS. Cooking Receipts from *Harper's Bazar*. 32mo, Paper, 25 cents.

PRACTICAL COOKING AND DINNER GIVING. A Treatise containing Practical Instructions in Cooking; in the Combination and Serving of Dishes; and in the Fashionable Modes of Entertaining at Breakfast, Lunch, and Dinner. By Mrs. Mary F. Henderson. Illustrated. 12mo, Cloth, $1 50.

SOCIAL ETIQUETTE AND HOME CULTURE. The Glass of Fashion: A Universal Hand-Book of Social Etiquette and Home Culture for Ladies and Gentlemen. With Copious and Practical Hints upon the Manners and Ceremonies of Every Relation in Life, at Home, in Society, and at Court. 4to, Paper, 20 cents.

YOUTH'S HEALTH BOOK. 32mo, Paper, 25 cents.

THE CARE OF PROPERTY. Hints to Women on the Care of Property. By Alfred Walker. 32mo, Paper, 20 cents.

THE ART OF BEAUTY. By Mrs. H. R. Haweis. With numerous Illustrations by the Author. Square 16mo, Cloth, Ornamental Cover, $1 75.

Published by HARPER & BROTHERS, New York.

☞ *Sent postage prepaid, to any part of the United States, on receipt of the price.*

www.ingramcontent.com/pod-product-compliance
Lightning Source LLC
Chambersburg PA
CBHW031815230426
43669CB00009B/1146